# Cambridge Elements ≡

Elements in Publishing and Book Culture
edited by
Samantha Rayner
*University College London*
Leah Tether
*University of Bristol*

# INTERNATIONAL BESTSELLERS AND THE ONLINE RECONFIGURING OF NATIONAL IDENTITY

Rachel Noorda

*Portland State University*

Millicent Weber

*Australian National University*

Melanie Ramdarshan Bold

*University of Glasgow*

CAMBRIDGE
UNIVERSITY PRESS

Shaftesbury Road, Cambridge CB2 8EA, United Kingdom

One Liberty Plaza, 20th Floor, New York, NY 10006, USA

477 Williamstown Road, Port Melbourne, VIC 3207, Australia

314–321, 3rd Floor, Plot 3, Splendor Forum, Jasola District Centre,
New Delhi – 110025, India

103 Penang Road, #05–06/07, Visioncrest Commercial, Singapore 238467

Cambridge University Press is part of Cambridge University Press & Assessment,
a department of the University of Cambridge.

We share the University's mission to contribute to society through the pursuit of
education, learning and research at the highest international levels of excellence.

www.cambridge.org
Information on this title: www.cambridge.org/9781009108485

DOI: 10.1017/9781009104388

First published 2024

*A catalogue record for this publication is available from the British Library.*

ISBN 978-1-009-10848-5 Paperback
ISSN 2514-8524 (online)
ISSN 2514-8516 (print)

Cambridge University Press & Assessment has no responsibility for the persistence
or accuracy of URLs for external or third-party internet websites referred to in this
publication and does not guarantee that any content on such websites is, or will
remain, accurate or appropriate.

# International Bestsellers and the Online Reconfiguring of National Identity

## Elements in Publishing and Book Culture

DOI: 10.1017/9781009104388

First published online: May 2024

Rachel Noorda

*Portland State University*

Millicent Weber

*Australian National University*

Melanie Ramdarshan Bold

*University of Glasgow*

Author for correspondence: Rachel Noorda, rnoorda@pdx.edu

ABSTRACT: International bestsellers are ideal sites for examining the complicated relationship between literary culture and national identity. Despite the transnational turns in both literary studies and book history, place is still an important configurer of twenty-first-century books' reception. Books are crucial to national identity and catalysts of nationalist movements. On an individual level, books enable readers to shape and maintain their own national identities. This Element explores how contemporary readers' understandings of nation, race/ethnicity, gender, and class continue to shape their reading, using as case studies the online reception of three bestselling titles – Liane Moriarty's *Big Little Lies* (Australia), Zadie Smith's *NW* (UK), and Kevin Kwan's *Crazy Rich Asians* (USA). In doing so, this Element demonstrates the need for and articulates a transnational conceptualisation of the relationship between reader identity and reception.

KEYWORDS: reception, national literatures, publishing, reading, anglophone

ISBNs: 9781009108485 (PB), 9781009104388 (OC)

ISSNs: 2514-8524 (online), 2514-8516 (print)

# Contents

# 1 Introduction

Envision for a moment three distinct twenty-first-century readers who, while situated in different parts of the world, are connected in their reading reception online through social media. We'll call these readers Jacob, Maria, and Diane.

Jacob is a white thirty-five-year-old man who lives in Amsterdam, where he works as a schoolteacher. He has recently read Zadie Smith's *NW*, a book set in London and written by a Black British author. While he has visited London once before on holiday, he has not been to North West London and enjoyed the educational experience of reading the book. Jacob read the book in his native language of Dutch.

Maria is a twenty-one-year-old Filipino university student living in Manila. In 2018, she went with some of her friends to see the film *Crazy Rich Asians*, which she thoroughly enjoyed. When she discovered that the film was based on a book by Kevin Kwan, she quickly bought the book and read it. While she didn't love everything about the book, she liked being able to talk about her opinions on it with friends both in person and online.

Diane is twenty-eight years old, non-binary, and living in Toronto, Canada. Their parents immigrated from China before Diane was born, so Diane identifies as Chinese Canadian. They have read a few books by the Australian author Liane Moriarty and so when they saw *Big Little Lies* in a local bookstore, they decided to purchase it. The book is set in Sydney, Australia, a place Diane has never been and does not know much about.

Jacob, Maria, and Diane all posted reviews of their reading experiences on the Amazon-owned social media site Goodreads. They all also navigate complicated identities at the intersections of self, nation, and literature, mediated through online platforms. Though Jacob, Maria, and Diane are not exact examples (for ethical data purposes) of the readers on Goodreads that this Element investigates, they are representative of the complexity of situated reading reception and identity in a globally connected and online environment.

The reading and identity practices of twenty-first-century readers across national contexts prompt a key question: what is the relationship between nations, identity, and literature? Not only do books circulate beyond geographical and national borders, but books are key to the construction of nations and national identity in the first place.[1] While global book networks and reading communities existed previously, the internet connects national book industries and readers in the twenty-first century in a manner and at a scale that is unprecedented. It's no wonder, then, that the examination of twenty-first-century book culture would necessitate a transnational approach that includes online spaces.[2]

National identity construction and maintenance are intertwined with book culture, meaning that readers are active participants in identity construction by engaging with and discussing texts embedded with ideologies. Engaging with these texts and by extension these ideologies challenges and/or reinforces the elements, ideas, and assumptions that have traditionally shaped collective understandings of nation and national literature. As book culture – which includes reading and reviewing books – becomes increasingly global, it is important to examine how national literatures are consecrated in online spaces in relation to shifts in forces and practices.

This Element investigates the relationship between the book and the nation in the twenty-first century. This relationship is characterised, on the one hand, by shifts from national to international modes of doing business, and by social and cultural interactions that take place in online, non-locationally confined fora, and, on the other, by growing conservative nationalism. The broad questions we seek to answer are both conceptual and methodological. What is the relationship between books and nations during the contemporary shifts

[1]  B. Anderson, *Imagined Communities: Reflections on the Origin and Spread of Nationalism* (Verso, 1983); A. Smith, *Ethno-symbolism and Nationalism: A Cultural Approach* (Routledge, 2009); E. Eisenstein, *The Printing Press As an Agent of Change* (Cambridge University Press, 1980); R. Noorda, 'From *Waverley* to *Outlander*: Reinforcing Scottish Diasporic Identity through Book Consumption', *National Identities* 20, no. 4 (2018): 361–77.

[2]  G. Sapiro, 'How Do Literary Works Cross Borders (Or Not)? A Sociological Approach to World Literature', *Journal of World Literature* 1, no. 1 (2016): 81–96; R. Fraser and M. Hammond, *Books without Borders, Volume 1: The Cross-National Dimension in Print Culture* (Palgrave Macmillan, 2008); P. Casanova, *The World Republic of Letters* (Harvard University Press, 2004); B. Driscoll and D. Rehberg Sedo, 'The Transnational Reception of Bestselling Books between Canada and Australia', *Global Media and Communication* 16, no. 2 (2020): 243–58.

towards international business models and social and cultural interactions as well as growing conservative nationalism? And how can we best explore this relationship? We explore these questions in our Element through analysis of reader responses to three case study titles. The three case studies are works of family-centred fiction from England,[3] the USA,[4] and Australia[5] that occupy contrasting positions in their own national literary fields and that have travelled, or not, to varying degrees, but which would all be considered bestsellers in sales terms. These texts are Zadie Smith's *NW*, Kevin Kwan's *Crazy Rich Asians*, and Liane Moriarty's *Big Little Lies*. Variously literary, middlebrow, and popular; urban, suburban, and international; and local and broad in their readerships, these texts offer several useful starting points to help us think through this intersection of identity and book culture, and they were chosen for their varied representation of key themes of wealth, class, ethnicity/race, and gender. Goodreads reviews of these texts complement our own

---

[3] Throughout this Element, 'United Kingdom' (UK) and 'Great Britain' will be used interchangeably, with 'British' used as a term for overarching locational identity in that region. However, whenever more specifics are possible (England/ English, Scotland/Scottish, Wales/Welsh, etc.) those terms will be used. National identity in the UK is very complex because it is a collective made up of four nations/national identities (England, Scotland, Wales, Northern Ireland).

[4] Throughout this Element, 'USA' is the term used over 'American', given that there are many people and national literatures on the North and South American continents beyond residents of the United States of America. However, there are a few instances when 'USA' could not be used for readability (such as when referring to Americans of Asian descent).

[5] Just as 'England' and 'USA' are pragmatic but not unproblematic terminological choices when it comes to discussing national identity, so too is 'Australia'. 'Australia' as a national construct is a product of British colonisation. As researchers, we acknowledge the distinct cultures and languages of hundreds of Aboriginal and Torres Strait Islander nations and pay our particular respects to the Ngunnawal and Ngambri people, who are the traditional custodians of the land on which the 'Australian' third of our research team is based. More information about the distinct Aboriginal and Torres Strait Islander nations and a map of Indigenous Australia can be found on the AIATSIS website: https://aiatsis.gov.au/ explore/map-indigenous-australia.

readings of the texts by providing the voice of the 'real reader', enabling us to investigate how different readers' national identity and other identities frame and interact with the text in the reading experience.[6]

## *Researching Books in the Twenty-First Century*

This research belongs to the discipline Rachel Noorda and Stevie Marsden describe as 'twenty-first-century book studies'.[7] This discipline is itself a contemporary-focused branch of book history, which is the study of 'those aspects of the book that have historically been seen as incidental to the main purpose of the book, which is to transmit ideas, but in fact crucially inform this process'.[8] In other words, the discipline of twenty-first-century book studies demonstrates a mixture of shared affinities with and departures from the methodologies and objects of study of book history and contemporary literary studies. It has become commonplace in twenty-first-century book studies to discuss the disruption caused by the publishing industry's conglomeration and globalisation and by the major technological advancements since the late twentieth century. These changes have had radical effects on the practices of writing, publishing, selling, and reading books, particularly in relation to the way that production, circulation, and reception are bound by the structure of the nation.

Historically, the nation has been homologous with a number of broad containers that tended to be placed around book industries – linguistic boundaries and legal and policy frameworks, for example – making the relationship between nation and print culture a pragmatic point of reference for contemporary book studies scholars. Indeed, the emergence of the modern nation state

[6] G. Hall, 'Texts, Readers – and Real Readers', *Language and Literature* 18, no. 3 (2009): 331–7; D. Fuller and D. Rehberg Sedo, *Reading beyond the Book: The Social Practices of Contemporary Literary Culture* (Routledge, 2013); I. Willis, *Reception* (Routledge, 2017).

[7] R. Noorda and S. Marsden, 'Twenty-First Century Book Studies: The State of the Discipline', *Book History* 22 (2019): 370–97.

[8] P. Henningsgaard, 'Emerging from the Rubble of Postcolonial Studies: Book History and Australian Literary Studies', *Ilha Do Desterro* 69, no. 2 (2016): 117–26 (p. 121).

is closely tied to the history of books. Just as the nation has historically influenced the circulation of books and other print material, said print culture has been central to the construction and dissemination of national (cultural) identities.[9] Wilkins, Driscoll, and Fletcher note that nationally bound book cultures and processes are still prominent even as the world continues to be more globally connected: 'National frameworks for the making and distribution of books are resilient, and we see no evidence of their imminent dissolution.' Three factors ensure this resilience: the way international property is carved geographically (region and nation), 'the persistent importance of live and in-person author events in book marketing', and niche subgenres that flourish in specific markets or regions but not in others.[10]

Indeed, despite the internationalising influences of industrial and technological disruptions, scholars like Wendy Griswold have argued that 'cultural regionalism, and regional literature in particular, is flourishing'.[11] This cultural reality has roots within a broader, somewhat paradoxical media context – namely, while individual expression, and indeed a celebration of individual diversity, is fostered by the openness of new technologies like social media, researchers have simultaneously demonstrated that the deregulated nature of these platforms also acts to bolster existing social and political structures by recreating communities built on narrow conceptions of identity. At its most extreme, this has played out as the growth of exclusionary and deeply normative online spaces: loci of xenophobic and patriarchal discourse.[12]

The transnational turn in contemporary literary studies has, particularly in relation to the methodologies of textual analysis, 'productively complicated the nationalist paradigm long dominant' in the discipline.[13] This work builds

---

[9] Anderson, *Imagined Communities*.

[10] K. Wilkins, B. Driscoll, and L. Fletcher, *Genre Worlds: Popular Fiction and 21st-Century Book Culture* (University of Massachusetts Press, 2022), p. 60.

[11] W. Griswold, *Regionalism and the Reading Class* (University of Chicago Press, 2008), p. 1.

[12] C. Tynan, 'Nationalism in the Age of Social Media', Temple Libraries' Scholars Studio Blog (13 December 2017).

[13] P. Jay, *Global Matters: The Transnational Turn in Literary Studies* (Cornell University Press, 2011), p. 1.

naturally on that of postcolonial studies scholars, which likewise seeks to 'challenge the primacy of discrete national literatures' and in doing so to provide 'a framework for studying literature and culture in a transnational context that moved beyond and explicitly questioned older Eurocentric models of "comparative" analysis'.[14] This transnational imperative is framed by similar shifts in broader, nationally framed disciplines like Australian studies or American studies, which in the twenty-first century, 'pay increasing attention to the historical roots of multidirectional flows of people, ideas, and goods and the social, political, linguistic, cultural, and economic crossroads generated in the process',[15] and through this seek to articulate how 'borderlands, crossroads, and contact zones . . . disrupt celebratory nationalist narratives'.[16] In other words, the transnational turn in contemporary literary studies has been an important and productive way to problematise and complicate national literature and the nation–literature relationship.

Robert Dixon's plan for 'a transnational practice of Australian literary criticism' provides one such example of this imperative.[17] Dixon advocated for research that would 'explore and elaborate the many ways in which the national literature has always been connected to the world', and – of particular note for book cultures and publishing studies scholarship – explicitly identified the study of publishing's economic and industry contexts, and of reception and reading formations, as among the six concrete strands of research key to this new practice.[18] David Carter, also writing from an Australian perspective, likewise describes a shift 'in the 1980s . . . from literary criticism to textual politics, [with] the current trend . . . from textual politics towards various forms of cultural history

---

[14] Jay, *Global Matters*, pp. 1–2.

[15] S. Fishkin, 'Crossroads of Cultures: The Transnational Turn in American Studies – Presidential Address to the American Studies Association, 12 November 2004', *American Quarterly* 57, no. 1 (2005): 17–57 (p. 22).

[16] Fishkin, 'Crossroads of Cultures', p. 19.

[17] R. Dixon, 'Australian Literature: International Contexts', *Southerly* 67, no. 1/2 (2007): 15–27 (p. 22).

[18] Dixon, 'Australian Literature: International Contexts', p. 20.

and print culture studies'[19] as part of a trend in literary scholarship that 'both expands and collapses the logics of literary postcolonialism'.[20] For scholars in twenty-first-century book studies or book history, these lines of enquiry are familiar territory.

Indeed, twenty-first-century book studies researchers have regularly demonstrated the importance of considering how books' production and circulation recombines or transcends nationalist conceptions of print culture. Explorations of books and other literary works in translations[21] or edited and repackaged international editions,[22] postcolonial studies of authorial self-positioning,[23] and analyses of literary prizes, festivals, and other mechanisms of prestige[24] interrogate how the production of books, as objects of cultural value, occurs within, beyond, and across national boundaries. The relationship between books and places, particularly in relation to how those books are represented in peritextual and epitextual materials,[25] is

---

[19] D. Carter, 'After Postcolonialism', *Meanjin* 66, no. 2 (2007): 114–19 (p. 118).

[20] Carter, 'After Postcolonialism', p. 119.

[21] See M. Jacklin, 'The Transnational Turn in Australian Literary Studies', *Journal of the Association for the Study of Australian Literature.* Special Issue: Australian Literature in a Global World (2009): 1–14; G. Whitlock and R. Osborne, 'Benang: A Worldly Book', *Journal of the Association for the Study of Australian Literature* 13, no. 3 (2013): 1–15.

[22] See P. Henningsgaard, 'The Editing and Publishing of Tim Winton in the United States', in *Tim Winton: Critical Essays*, edited by L. McCredden and N. O'Reilly, pp. 122–60 (UWA Publishing, 2014).

[23] See S. Brouillette, *Postcolonial Writers in the Global Literary Marketplace* (Palgrave Macmillan, 2007); M. Ramdarshan Bold, *Inclusive Young Adult Fiction: Authors of Colour in the United Kingdom* (Palgrave Pivot, 2019).

[24] See S. Pickford, 'The Booker Prize and the Prix Goncourt: A Case Study of Award-Winning Novels in Translation', *Book History* 14 (2011): 221–40; S. Ponzanesi, *The Postcolonial Cultural Industry: Icons, Markets, Mythologies* (Palgrave Macmillan UK, 2014); M. Weber, *Literary Festivals and Contemporary Book Culture* (Palgrave Macmillan, 2018).

[25] G. Genette, *Paratexts: Thresholds of Interpretation* (Cambridge University Press, 1997).

further complicated when digital and audio formats are considered in conjunction with print.[26]

## Transnational Reception: Situated Reading

Despite the transnational turns in both literary studies and book history, place is still an important constructor of twenty-first-century book reception. As James Procter and Bethan Benwell found in their research with book groups around the world, 'Place anchors and orientates readers and groups in relation to the book at hand, helping them to establish and explain proximal alignments, or feelings of detachment, generating expressions of textual familiarity or foreignness, identification or isolation'.[27] In this way, readers use location as a means to 're-evaluate and question their own place in the world'.[28] Interpreting these practices requires that 'reading itself needs to be understood as a situated rather than a straightforwardly transhistorical or translocational act'.[29]

We take up the language of 'situation' that Procter and Benwell use as the backbone of our argument in this Element: *that twenty-first-century reading is triply situated*. We see reading as situated (1) within the self, (2) within the nation, and (3) within the online environment. Not only does each context matter in its own right, they are also intertwined, particularly for reading communities of individuals across national boundaries who convene reading and review practices online.

Reading is situated within the 'self' of the reader. In order to understand reading as a situated, individual act, we need to conduct empirical research into the practices of real readers, and this empiricism is a central tenet of the history of reading and of book history more generally.[30] For example,

---

[26] P. Henningsgaard, 'Ebooks, Book History, and Markers of Place', *Logos* 30, no. 1 (6 June 2019): 31–44.

[27] J. Procter and B. Benwell, *Reading across Worlds: Transnational Book Groups and the Reception of Difference* (Palgrave Macmillan, 2014), p. 52.

[28] Procter and Benwell, *Reading across Worlds*, p. 72.

[29] Procter and Benwell, *Reading across Worlds*, p. 3.

[30] See D. Miall, 'Empirical Approaches to Studying Literary Readers: The State of the Discipline', *Book History* 9 (2006): 291–311.

Gillian Whitlock and Roger Osborne note, in their book historical study of the international transit of Kim Scott's *Benang*, that 'Although we can read the physical metamorphoses of the travelling book from changes in livery and paratexts, [it] is difficult to gain an understanding of the reception of Indigenous writing in Europe without quantitative and qualitative studies.'[31] Robert Fraser and Mary Hammond claim that investigating the intersection of nation with book production and reception cannot be 'aired in a cosy literary-critical setting' because the 'materialities of production and the realities of reception ... serve to position [this research]'.[32] This Element leverages the wealth of empirical data about reading practices available online in order to examine the twenty-first-century reality of books' international reception. How and why do books resonate with multiple, international audiences? And how can we productively investigate the nexus of reader identity and books' reception? Our Element seeks to explore these questions.

Twenty-first-century reading remains situated within the nation. Our project builds on other scholarship that explores the relationship between books and nationhood. For example, *Books without Borders* asks 'Where does the book belong?' in national, international, and transnational contexts.[33] Gisèle Sapiro attempts to address the factors involved in the 'circulation of literary works beyond their geographical and cultural borders'.[34] However, studies like these either ignore the twenty-first century entirely or claim to describe the contemporary situation without considering key factors in twenty-first-century reception such as the internet, social media, or digital book forms. Many of these studies take a top-down approach to book culture in order to measure the social factors or international standing of a book, rather than using real social interactions and situations in the twenty-first century, such as those on social media or those taking place at festivals and events.

---

[31] Whitlock and Osborne, 'Benang', p. 6.

[32] Fraser and Hammond, *Books without Borders*, p. 3.

[33] Fraser and Hammond, *Books without Borders*.

[34] Sapiro, 'How Do Literary Works Cross Borders (Or Not)?', p. 81.

In the contemporary environment, geographical, social, and cultural models for nations no longer easily map on to one another. Wilkins, Driscoll, and Fletcher, in *Genre Worlds*, acknowledge the complexity of mapping the local, regional, national, and global in twenty-first-century publishing. These authors found that their interviewees understood how their own national context was part of a connected global genre 'but not fully contained by it'.[35] Additionally, more prestigious cultural forms (like literary fiction) are often associated with national or regional structures, while mass culture (like genre fiction) is associated with the global. The reality is much more complicated, though, hence these authors' observation that genre fiction is both global and national. *Genre Worlds* addresses the traditional movement of texts that spring from national to international context as starting in the periphery and pulled towards the centre to increase commercial success and validation.[36] However, these authors found that in addition to the pull of the centre, there is lateral movement between small or medium national markets, such as Australia and Germany.[37]

Beth Driscoll and DeNel Rehberg Sedo found similar lateral movement between the two smaller markets of Australia and Canada. Driscoll and Rehberg Sedo's work on transnational reception of books between Canada and Australia takes a twenty-first-century approach, studying real agents, situations, and interactions around key case study titles. Their methodology focuses on identifying a set of Australian and Canadian case study titles from bestseller lists in a ten-year period and then investigating their publishing histories, rights sales, prizes and adaptations, and reception in print media and online. This grounded perspective uses rich quantitative and qualitative data to develop theoretical underpinnings. Driscoll and Rehberg Sedo find a 'diversity of actors in the ecosystem of a transnational bestseller' in which concentrated power of the largest publishers is not total. Additionally, these authors find there is no one-size-fits-all story or strategy for becoming a transnational bestseller but 'instead, there are various

---

[35] Wilkins, Driscoll, and Fletcher, *Genre Worlds*, p. 59.

[36] Wilkins, Driscoll, and Fletcher, *Genre Worlds*, p. 64.

[37] Driscoll and Rehberg Sedo, 'The Transnational Reception of Bestselling Books', pp. 254–5.

currents at work, influenced by factors including the date of a book's publication, the intersecting activities of small press and multinational conglomerates in its publishing trajectory, its uptake by different media institutions, and the genre of the book and the kinds of readers and media that the genre attracts'.[38] Thus, Driscoll and Rehberg Sedo's research illustrates the complicated web of agents, situations, and interactions that impact a book's transnational reception.

However, Driscoll and Rehberg Sedo still frame markets as either central or peripheral, highlighting the peripheral nature of the Canadian and Australian markets, eclipsed and mediated by markets in the USA and UK. While the USA and UK book markets wield great power in the global literary sphere, we want to break open the central–peripheral binary, particularly when discussing readers in the online reading space. Pascale Casanova's *World Republic of Letters*, while offering a foundational remapping of the international literary space, is rooted in the idea that the interlinked national literary economies are either central or located on the periphery.[39] But in online communities in the twenty-first century, all communities are simultaneously central and peripheral at once. Individuals' relationships to the nation and the world are different in this environment and thus require flagging, concealing, or negotiating in various ways. An understanding of what nation actually means for people as readers in the twenty-first century must take online communities and new reading practices into consideration. In other words, reading is now situated in a-locational or translocational online contexts at the same time as it is deeply located through its situation in self and in the nation.

Taken in this sense, we describe reading in the twenty-first century as post-digital.[40] We understand analog, digital, and physically embodied engagement with books and book culture not as polar opposites but as commingled. We likewise understand social engagement with a 'digital'

---

[38] Driscoll and Rehberg Sedo, 'The Transnational Reception of Bestselling Books', p. 254.

[39] Casanova, *The World Republic of Letters*.

[40] F. Cramer, 'What Is "Post-Digital"?' In *Postdigital Aesthetics: Art, Computation and Design*, edited by D. M. Berry and M. Dieter, pp. 12–26 (Palgrave Macmillan, 2015).

environment or community not to be a derivative or representation of a 'true' interaction, but a form of engagement with one among many spaces in which individuals' identities are socially and culturally constructed and performed. We see the injunction to study online reading as particularly imperative when 'traditional' print reading practices are happening alongside and vying for space with other forms of mediated reading. At this moment, understanding the ways in which readers interact with online communities alongside and through their reading is crucial to understanding the future of book culture.

This Element is structured into four sections. Section 1, 'Introduction', has established the focus of this Element and in particular the need for an investigation of national and transnational contexts for online reading. We situate our work within the framework of twenty-first-century book studies and lay the groundwork for our argument: that contemporary reading needs to be understood as triply situated. Section 2, 'Methodology: Reading the Reader, Online', locates our research in online reader response and reception and details the close and comparative analysis and online reviews of our case study texts. We use this approach because it enables us to examine the relationship between textual representation and readers' understanding of identity. This methodology supports and is supported by our contention that reading is situated in the self of the reader, the nation, and the online environment. Section 3, 'Multiply Situated Reading in Practice', presents our results along four main themes: representation/misrepresentation, genre and gender identity, the author–reader relationship, and adaptation and format. These themes emerged from our close reading of the case study texts and our multistage analysis of their online reviews. Finally, we bring together these lines of enquiry in Section 4, 'Conclusion', where we return to our research questions, evaluating the extent to which our analysis can resolve the tricky relationship between identity and book reading as we shift deeper into the twenty-first century, and discussing potentially productive further research in this regard. Ultimately, we find that readers' adherence to nationality sits in conjunction with expressions of and adherence to other facets of their identity. Each is called upon in contingent and unequal ways to inform and shape the reading experience. The relationship between books, reading, and national identity is subject to a complex push-and-pull in the contested and sometimes politicised landscape of contemporary book culture.

## 2 Methodology: Reading the Reader, Online

Scholars of reading have traditionally explored readers' acts of meaning-making, or interpretation. These acts occur by means of personal encounters or transactions between reader and text,[41] which are shaped by readers' backgrounds and knowledge, and the embedding of the reader and/or reading experience within a range of social institutions.[42] Scholars like David Miall have argued that one of the rationales for empirical accounts of reading is their ability to negotiate between these contrasting experiences and social institutions. Experimental approaches to the study of reading are particularly prized: 'no doubt the study of published interpretations has its own merit, but it is a poor answer to the question of how texts are actually read'.[43] This question of 'how texts are actually read' offers a kind of value proposition for research into reading: it provides information about what real readers think and do when they encounter books, in distinction to 'published interpretations' in particular, which are by contrast seen as subject to filters and prior conceptions that distort the picture of reading they can offer. This drives a need for further reception studies research that listens to the 'real reader' rather than focusing purely on the 'implied' or intended reader.[44]

Research that explores the digital traces of reception has an indeterminate status in relation to this rationale and critique. Online conversations about books certainly provide access to a range of readers, trained and untrained and from various demographic groups, rather than only highly educated professional readers, but these conversations are still embedded in a vast range of social, technological, and political infrastructures.[45] Indeed,

[41] L. Rosenblatt, 'The Literary Transaction: Evocation and Response', *Theory into Practice* 21, no. 4 (1982): 268–77.

[42] M. de Certeau, 'Reading As Poaching', in *The Practice of Everyday Life*, translated by S. Rendall, pp. 165–76 (University of California Press, 1984); S. Fish, *Is There a Text in This Class? The Authority of Interpretive Communities* (Harvard University Press, 1980).

[43] Miall, 'Empirical Approaches to Studying Literary Readers', p. 292.

[44] Willis, *Reception*.

[45] D. Allington, '"Power to the Reader" or "Degradation of Literary Taste"? Professional Critics and Amazon Customers As Reviewers of *The Inheritance of*

this question of 'how texts are actually read' is not the primary question that we are concerned with, for several reasons. Putting aside major epistemic scruples, are not all readings intrinsically mediated by any process of communicating about them, whether that be written, spoken, or reported in some other way? Does this communicative process not in fact construct readings? Our interest is less in what happens at that moment when readers interact with books, and more in the social and cultural practices that surround books. Essentially, we ask how and why people, both individually and collectively, perceive, interact with, and interact because of books.

Platforms like Goodreads, the major 'site' of our 'fieldwork' for this Element, are public, sociable, enormous, and commercially mediated.[46] They are consequently important spaces in which these bookish practices take place. This is particularly true in our contemporary, post-digital context.[47] Like other internet users, twenty-first-century readers are 'self-reflexively multimodal',[48] and such 'transmedia practices and trans-literate multimodal readers put pressure on the older ideas of readers as either individuated subjects or collectives'.[49] The readers we are studying are not readers by virtue of picking up, thumbing through, and inter-preting stitched-up assemblages of paper and ink; they are readers

*Loss', Language and Literature* 25, no. 3 (1 August 2016): 254–78; Fuller and Rehberg Sedo, *Reading beyond the Book.*

[46] The commercially mediated nature of Goodreads is even more evident since its purchase by Amazon in 2013: R. Deahl and J. Milliot, 'Amazon Buys Goodreads', *Publishers Weekly*, 28 March 2013.

[47] C. Berry, S. Kim, and L. Spigel, *Electronic Elsewheres: Media, Technology, and the Experience of Social Space* (University of Minnesota Press, 2010); S. Pink and K. Mackley, 'Saturated and Situated: Expanding the Meaning of Media in the Routines of Everyday Life', *Media, Culture & Society* 35, no. 6 (1 September 2013): 677–91.

[48] D. Fuller, 'The Multimodal Reader: Or, How My Obsession with NRK's Skam Made Me Think Again about Readers, Reading and Digital Media', *Participations: Journal of Audience and Reception Studies* 16, no. 1 (2019): 496–509 (p. 497).

[49] Fuller, 'The Multimodal Reader', p. 506.

because they actively identify as such through participation in these big public book cultures.[50] While this Element focuses on Goodreads as the largest and most popular book-related social media platform, many alternatives, including LibraryThing (2005) and StoryGraph (2019), are available.

## Goodreads Reviews

Simone Murray calls Goodreads 'the world's dominant book-centric social networking and cataloguing platform',[51] which 'indisputably dominates online literary sociability'.[52] At the time of writing in 2023, Goodreads' most recent advertising documentation claims the site has 125 million members, 3.5 billion books, and 110 million reviews.[53] In her analysis, Murray cautions researchers against the allure of Goodreads data that don't take into account 'the limited extent to which users either understand or can influence its algorithmic operations, leading to overblown claims of readerly empowerment'.[54] Crucially, then, a twenty-first-century book studies analysis of Goodreads reviews needs to take into account both agency and algorithm, balancing reader choice and platform influence. Therefore, we seek to acknowledge that algorithms are at work in the readerly experiences and data collection via Goodreads. These algorithms limit the number of Goodreads reviews researchers can collect and the order in which they can collect them. The reviewers on Goodreads are not only engaging in a social sharing of book recommendations with friends; they are entrenched in an Amazon-owned system in which amateur reviews are commoditised and monetised, such as through the Review

---

[50] N. Rodger, 'From Bookshelf Porn and Shelfies to #bookfacefriday: How Readers Use Pinterest to Promote Their Bookishness', *Participations: Journal of Audience and Reception Studies* 16, no. 1 (2019): 473–94.

[51] S. Murray, 'Secret Agents: Algorithmic Culture, Goodreads and Datafication of the Contemporary Book World', *European Journal of Cultural Studies* 24, no. 4 (2021): 970–89 (p. 973).

[52] Murray, 'Secret Agents', p. 977.

[53] Goodreads, 'Book Discovery Information Kit', n.d.

[54] Murray, 'Secret Agents', p. 972.

Partner Program in which publishers pay for Goodreads reviews. Goodreads also uses demographic and behavioural data about its users so as to inform targeted advertising campaigns. The typical Goodreads user has been described as 'a 25- to 34-year old, US-based Caucasian,[55] graduate educated woman with children, a median income of USA $100,000–150,000, who watches MSNBC and PBS, and enjoys science programmes'.[56] Goodreads' own most recent publicly circulated demographic information, collected by the Quantcast market research service in 2021 and shared on request with advertisers, shows similar findings, although the audience is now older. Quantcast estimates that 70 per cent of Goodreads' users are women, 43 per cent have an income higher than USA $100,000, 34 per cent are between 35 and 54 years old (compared to 23 per cent who are 25–34, the next most common age group), virtually all users are college graduates with 30 per cent completing some kind of graduate school as well, and 220 million of the 435 million monthly page views come from USA-based users.[57]

Beth Driscoll and DeNel Rehberg Sedo have described Goodreads as 'a complex site', in reference both to the site's own mechanics and to its role within a complex book culture ecosystem.[58] Participants in this ecosystem:

> add books to virtual shelves, allocate them star ratings, write and reply to reviews, follow one another, and participate in discussion forums. There are links out to personal and commercial websites. Readers who use a Kindle (another Amazon technology) are prompted to add purchased books to their Goodreads account, and rate them when they finish reading. Within this constellation of digital book-based practices,

---

[55] Just to note, the term 'Caucasian' is outdated, problematic, and rooted in the racist historical science of racial classification.

[56] J. Cheney-Lippold, 'A New Algorithmic Identity: Soft Biopolitics and the Modulation of Control', *Theory, Culture & Society* 28, no. 6 (2011): 164–81 (p. 165).

[57] Goodreads, 'Book Discovery Information Kit'.

[58] B. Driscoll and D. Rehberg Sedo, 'Faraway, So Close: Seeing the Intimacy in Goodreads Reviews', *Qualitative Inquiry* 25, no. 3 (1 March 2019): 248–59 (p. 250).

reviews form a distinct reading response. Not every kind of reader writes online reviews, and the millions who do occupy a specific position in book culture. The reviews they write are significant for researchers because they provide access to a kind of reading experience that has previously been elusive. This opportunity is offset by difficulty; the size of Goodreads makes it harder to appreciate and contextualise the richness and complexity of individual reviews. In particular, it can be difficult for researchers to see intimacy when it is enmeshed in big data and new technological infrastructure.[59]

Like other researchers studying online reading practices, we assert the value of paying attention to readers and to their own statements about reading as a methodological technique.[60] Driscoll and Rehberg Sedo have argued that taking seriously such a commitment 'informed by feminist standpoint epistemology . . . enables researchers to recognize the agency of these readers, and analyze their relation to the social and cultural institutions that legitimize certain types of reading'.[61] In exploring how identity and book readership relate in an online, twenty-first-century context, we analyse the extent to which key facets of national identity – namely, social class, ethnicity/race, wealth, and gender, as well as the representation of place – are present in each of our case study texts, and in the reviews of those texts on Goodreads. As noted, our case study texts – *NW*, *Crazy Rich Asians*, and *Big Little Lies* – fit certain broad parameters

---

[59] Driscoll and Rehberg Sedo, 'Faraway, So Close', pp. 248–259 (p. 250).

[60] Allington, '"Power to the Reader" or "Degradation of Literary Taste"?';
E. Finn, 'Revenge of the Nerd: Junot Díaz and the Networks of American Literary Imagination', *Digital Humanities Quarterly* 7, no. 1 (1 July 2013);
A. Steiner, 'Private Criticism in the Public Space: Personal Writing on Literature in Readers' Reviews on Amazon', *Participations: Journal of Audience and Reception Studies* 52, no. 2 (2008); A. Gruzd and D. Rehberg Sedo, '#1b1t: Investigating Reading Practices at the Turn of the Twenty-First Century', *Mémoires Du Livre* 3, no. 2 (8 June 2012).

[61] Driscoll and Rehberg Sedo, 'Faraway, So Close', pp. 248–9.

for selection: representation from and border-crossing between the three anglophone markets, categorisation as 'bestsellers' in multiple markets, varied depictions of key themes (wealth, social class, ethnicity/race, and gender), and within similar genre worlds/realms and types of readership communities.

There is one text each from the UK, the US, and Australia, which gives a window into three major anglophone publishing markets and allows comparison of books and identities travelling between the three countries. Each book was first published within two years of each other: *NW* in 2012, *Crazy Rich Asians* in 2013, and *Big Little Lies* in 2014. Publication date proximity is important because it allows the texts and their readership to be more comparable since they are operating in a similar moment in the publishing market, which is constantly changing. The three texts fit the definition of bestseller as given by Beth Driscoll and Claire Squires: 'Bestsellers are high-profile products that drive publishing as an industry and connect it to other media sectors', making bestsellers 'the public face of the industry' (Driscoll and Squires 2020, p. 6). These three texts draw large readerships and not just from traditional 'readers'. Their bestseller status has led to other media adaptations in TV and film, and review and discussion of the various forms of the content have encouraged public discourse about national identity, race, wealth, and gender. *NW*, *Crazy Rich Asians*, and *Big Little Lies* fit into a genre world we call family-centred fiction. Family-centred fiction overlaps and intersects with other genre designations such as chick lit, women's fiction, or Asian American fiction. Wilkins, Driscoll, and Fletcher define genre worlds as 'a collection of people and practices that operates, according to established and emerging patterns of collaborative activity, in order to produce the texts that make popular genres recognizable'.[62] Genre worlds offer a shorthand of expectations between reader and writer, have insiders and outsiders, and have three layers (industrial, social, and textual). This research addresses the industrial aspects of the family-centred fiction genre world through analysis of the publishing dynamics and mechanisms that make publication and promotion for the three books possible; social aspects of the reading communities that inhabit this genre world, especially in their

---

[62] Wilkins, Driscoll, and Fletcher, *Genre Worlds*, p. 2.

reviews and interactions online via Goodreads; and textual aspects through close readings and content analysis of the books and reviews for *NW*, *Crazy Rich Asians*, and *Big Little Lies*.

These are the specific reasons we have chosen *NW*, *Crazy Rich Asians*, and *Big Little Lies* as the case study texts for this Element. Our methodology is a comparative case study approach, which is particularly useful for social research about practice and industry.[63] Comparative case studies are contextualised within the broader social, political, cultural, economic, and national contexts in which practices (like reading) take place and develop. A case study methodology is especially appropriate for this research because it allows in-depth exploration of transnational publishing and reading examples within national contexts and identities. Yin defines a case study as 'an empirical inquiry that investigates a contemporary phenomenon (the case) in-depth and within its real-world context'.[64] Using empirical data from Goodreads, we investigate the contemporary phenomenon of national identity in the reception of family-centred fiction through three specific cases that are considered within their real-world contexts of publishing and reading.

We have explored these texts in three ways. Firstly, we have used textual analysis to benchmark how identity is represented in the text, based on our own critical readings as well as with respect to publication information and published reviews for each text. Secondly, using the program Outwit Hub, we have collated reviewer demographic information for the three titles based on the publicly viewable reviews on Goodreads. And thirdly, also using Outwit Hub, we have collated the text of these publicly viewable reviews (approximately 1,500 reviews for each title), and used word-frequency analysis to inform a targeted thematic analysis of their content.

Goodreads offers rich qualitative and quantitative data in the forms of both user-generated content and user statistics. For these case studies, we have considered the ethics and protocols of researching online

[63] L. Bartlett and F. Vavrus, *Rethinking Case Study Research: A Comparative Approach* (Taylor & Francis, 2016).

[64] R. Yin, *Case Study Research: Design and Methods* (Sage, 2009), p. 18.

communities, particularly around issues such as privacy and anonymity.[65] We have drawn upon the Association of Internet Researchers' (AOIR) (2019) guidelines, which differentiate between information that is publicly available and information that is sought from closed groups or private online communities, as well as the work of Langer and Beckman, which adopts established research ethics used for content analysis (e.g. of reader letters in newspapers) in public media.[66] As such, we view these online reviews as public documents but have also taken measures to remove identifying information.[67] The majority of the data about group members has been aggregated, anonymised, and included in the analysis. However, since Goodreads reviews are publicly available, we have included a limited number of direct quotes, paraphrased information as much as possible, and have not linked these to any specific Goodreads users.[68] This follows the same ethics strategy of Driscoll and Rehberg Sedo, who 'consider these publicly visible reviews to be acts of communication available for analysis' but also work to protect user privacy by not citing usernames in quotes.[69]

## *Digital National Identity*

Goodreads offers a site of interaction between the types of situatedness of the reader: self, nation, and online. The self situates the reader as informed by identities of class, race, and gender; these identities impact how readers interact with other readers because of books. The nation situates the reader in

[65] R. Ackland, *Web Social Science: Concepts, Data and Tools for Social Scientists in the Digital Age* (Sage, 2013); L. Sugiura, R. Wiles, and C. Pope, 'Ethical Challenges in Online Research: Public/Private Perceptions', *Research Ethics* 13, no. 3–4 (2017): 184–99.

[66] R. Langer and S. Beckman, 'Sensitive Research Topics: Netnography Revisited', *Qualitative Market Research* 8, no. 2 (2005): 189–203.

[67] R. Wiles, *What Are Qualitative Research Ethics?* (Bloomsbury Academic, 2013).

[68] N. Hookway, '"Entering the Blogosphere": Some Strategies for Using Blogs in Social Research', *Qualitative Research* 8, no. 1 (2008): 91–113; H. Smith, T. Dinev, and H. Xu, 'Information Privacy Research: An Interdisciplinary Review', *MIS Quarterly* 35, no. 4 (2011): 989–1016.

[69] Driscoll and Rehberg Sedo, 'Faraway, So Close', p. 251.

the community and culture of the reader's own national identity and awareness of national contexts for other readers, authors, and characters. The book industry is also still situated primarily on a national level, with transnational movement. Finally, Goodreads as a social media site situates the reader online. This section addresses the intersectional situatedness of digital national identity, aligning with a subfield within sociological national identities research.

Despite the global interconnectedness provided by the internet, national identities have not become less important. In fact, the internet and social media offer 'new channels and avenues thanks to which national identity not only has not disappeared, but, on the contrary, has been "re-embedded" and can flourish'.[70] Social media can be a fruitful site, therefore, for digital national identity scholarship,[71] especially in studying the everyday performance of national identity that Billig calls 'banal' nationalism.[72] Thus everyday national identity comes through in reviews on the social media site Goodreads, examined in this Element. One of the benefits of social media as a site of digital national identity performance and maintenance is that they provide a bottom-up approach to national identity, and in the case of Goodreads, allow researchers to listen to real readers.

Digital national identity is defined as 'self-identification with and a sense of belonging to the nation created, recreated and expressed online'.[73] Primarily digital national identity is another site for banal and everyday national identity performance, formation, and reinforcement. But in addition to being a site of everyday national identity, there are structural elements of the internet that perpetuate situatedness in a national context – for example, website domain

---

[70] P. Ahmad, 'Digital Nationalism As an Emergent Subfield of Nationalism Studies: The State of the Field and Key Issues', *National Identities* 24, no. 4 (2022): 307–17 (p. 308).

[71] H. Stratoudaki, 'Greek National Identity on Twitter: Re-negotiating Markers and Boundaries', *National Identities* 24, no. 4 (2022): 319–335; X. Li and J. Feng, 'Security and Digital Nationalism: Speaking the Brand of Australia on Social Media', *Media International Australia* (2022).

[72] M. Billig, *Banal Nationalism* (Sage, 1995).

[73] Ahmad, "Digital Nationalism As an Emergent Subfield of Nationalism Studies', p. 310.

names (such as .uk or .cn), nationally biased algorithms, and national digital ecosystems.[74]

Various aspects of identity also intersect, meaning that a reader's national identity intersects with and is performed with other identities. Stratoudaki puts it this way: 'In day-by-day reality, national and other identities mix, become crystalized or fluid as the sociopolitical environment calls for performing them.'[75] As our content analysis of Goodreads reviews for three case study texts reveals, other identities of gender, race, and class mix with national identity for readers as they discuss *NW*, *Crazy Rich Asians*, and *Big Little Lies*. Not only are these identities mixed (national identities and others), but they are also complex and in dialogue with each other.[76]

This Element takes up Ahmad's call to study 'how social media users express and utilize national identity online'.[77] This is accomplished through the analysis of Goodreads reviews around the three case study texts from the UK, the USA, and Australia. Through this particular methodology and the findings it prompts, we add to the scholarly conversations around online reader reception and digital national identity.

Twenty-first-century reading is situated in the nation. Shared language and national regulatory contexts are the sociopolitical building blocks that enable books to circulate. But the nation is also situated in literature: the nation is an imaginative and a social construct just as it is a geopolitical one. This section has detailed the methodology of this Element, which takes a bottom-up approach to online reader reception/response and digital national identities. In the next section, we hold the different facets of this big-picture conceptualisation of nation, identity, and literature up to our case study texts and their online reception. In doing so we examine the extent to which this continues to hold true in an online context.

[74] S. Mihelj and C. Jiménez-Martínez, 'Digital Nationalism: Understanding the Role of Digital Media in the Rise of "New" Nationalism', *Nations and Nationalism* 27, no. 2 (2021): 331–46 (p. 335).

[75] Stratoudaki, 'Greek National Identity on Twitter', p. 320.

[76] Stratoudaki, 'Greek National Identity on Twitter', p. 329.

[77] Ahmad,' Digital Nationalism As an Emergent Subfield of Nationalism Studies', p. 312.

# 3 Multiply Situated Reading in Practice

## *Reading the Case Study Texts*

### Crazy Rich Asians

The first of our case study texts, *Crazy Rich Asians*, was published in 2013 in the United States by Knopf Doubleday (an imprint of Penguin Random House). In 2014, it was published in Australia by Allen & Unwin and in the UK by Corvus (an imprint of the independent publisher Atlantic Books). The film adaptation of *Crazy Rich Asians* was released in 2018 and was notably lauded for its status as the first Hollywood movie to feature a cast of all East and Southeast Asian actors since the film adaptation of Amy Tan's *The Joy Luck Club* twenty-five years earlier.

Written by Singaporean American author Kevin Kwan, *Crazy Rich Asians* positions Asian American identity in a way rarely seen in the USA literary canon. The novel portrays the perspectives of several characters, with the most prominent of these protagonists Rachel Chu. Rachel is Chinese American, while the novel is mainly set in Singapore (with the US, Paris, London, and Australia also featured). Rachel is a foreigner to Singapore while she is also othered as part of a racially minoritized group in the USA: she both belongs and does not in each context. One of the key themes Kwan's story investigates is how Asian American identity is distinctive from national and ethnic identities in East and Southeast Asian countries like Singapore. As Nancy Wang Yuen noted in an article by *The Washington Post*'s Allyson Chiu, 'The Hollywood trope is to cast a white person as an "outsider" in Asia, but I think that they don't understand Asian Americans also feel like an outsider in Asia. We are every bit as American as a white person, especially if we were born and raised in the United States.'[78] Crucially, ancestry and racial ties do not make an Asian American character like Rachel Chu feel at home in Singapore. This positioning has enabled this bestselling book to investigate how wealth structures identity and social relations regardless of racial/ethnic and national identity.

---

[78] A. Chiu, 'Is *Crazy Rich Asians* Historic? "That's Just Way Too Much Pressure," Says Kevin Kwan, Who Wrote the Book', *The Washington Post*, 13 August 2018.

Social class and capitalism are key themes in the novel, especially as these themes are explored across national boundaries in a diasporic community. Ding calls *Crazy Rich Asians* both a 'neoliberal multicultural' and 'postcolonial capitalist' narrative that centres on Sinophone capitalism. Ding asserts: 'Kwan identifies and popularises a new postcolonial capitalist Sinophone identity buttressed by the consumption of western cultural and consumer products.'[79] The characters identify with and are defined by their consumption habits, which are primarily of Euro-American goods. As a neoliberal multicultural narrative, *Crazy Rich Asians* illustrates wealth as a vehicle to overthrow racism in some respects while cultivating racism in other ways. For example, the opening scene of the text features a young Nick with his mother, Eleanor, and aunt and cousin as they attempt to check into a hotel in the UK. The group is met with snobbery and racism from the white man at the front desk, which is then subverted once Eleanor reveals her wealth by calling her husband and buying the hotel. However, the novel also shows characters' racist views towards brown Malay and Indian Singaporeans, as well as tasteless 'new money' consumers from Mainland China and Taiwan.[80] The setting of Singapore for the novel offers a context that features the interaction of different East and Southeast Asian cultures overlayed on a history steeped in colonialism. For example, Singapore's colonial history (the country was a British colony until 1965) underpins the preference of the characters in the novel towards British English and British universities. Ding states, 'For Kwan's Singaporean elites, the only commodity more sought after than designer luxury brands is a British public school education and a perfect Queen's English, both of which serve to prove the old money's superiority.'[81]

Reviewers have argued that *Crazy Rich Asians* breaks from common tropes about Asian American characters (like being smart or good at martial

---

[79] Y. Ding, '"Asian Pride Porn": Neoliberal Multiculturalism and the Narrative of Asian Racial Uplift in Kevin Kwan's Crazy Rich Asians Trilogy', *MELUS* 45, no. 3 (2020): 65–82 (p. 68).

[80] H. Ellis-Pedersen and L. Kou, 'Where Are All the Brown People? Crazy Rich Asians Draws Tepid Response in Singapore', *The Guardian*, 21 August 2018.

[81] Ding, '"Asian Pride Porn"', p. 74.

arts) and likewise moves away from the 'model minority' stereotype. Kwan describes how his characters 'are presented as modern, cultured, even sexualized individuals who have zero baggage about their race'.[82] Although Kwan saw the Asian American readership as skeptical of *Crazy Rich Asians* at first, many readers have expressed gratitude that they could read about successful, attractive, and progressive characters. In *The Atlantic*, Alexander Abad-Santos applauds the way that *Crazy Rich Asians* goes beyond the common poor immigrant story (like in *The Joy Luck Club*) of the 'ambitious, well-behaved immigrant' to the many other sides of the Asian American experience, although likewise arguing that the work of 'serious' writers like Tan, Chang Rae-Lee, and Adeline Mah was necessary to pave the way for 'playful' stories like Kwan's.[83] On the other hand, Patricia Park, writing for *The Guardian*, accuses *Crazy Rich Asians* of still playing into Asian American character tropes, including framing the main character as a beautiful and incredibly smart (and accomplished) woman who exemplifies the stereotypical East and Southeast Asian bride-to-be: 'for all the stereotypes [*Crazy Rich Asians*] exposes then skewers, there are others peddled so earnestly that the reader can't help but wonder at Kwan's agenda'.[84]

*Crazy Rich Asians* has also been celebrated for – and Kwan himself has described his achievements as – crossing over into the 'exclusive genre' of 'chick lit'.[85] This has been lauded as another breaking down of barriers – significant because, in Patricia Park's words, 'A male author – an Asian one at that – has pushed past the velvet ropes of race, culture and gender, to tap that exclusive genre: chick lit.'[86] This celebration of Kwan's achievements

---

[82] A. Abad-Santos, 'Why Asians Love *Crazy Rich Asians*', *The Atlantic*, 4 September 2013.

[83] Abad-Santos, 'Why Asians Love *Crazy Rich Asians*'.

[84] P. Park, '*Crazy Rich Asians* Presents a Whole New Wave of Stereotypes', *The Guardian*, 3 September 2013.

[85] Park, '*Crazy Rich Asians* Presents a Whole New Wave of Stereotypes'; see also R. Sun, '*Crazy Rich Asians* Author Kevin Kwan: "Why Does Hollywood Think We'd Want to See This Movie with White People?"' *The Hollywood Reporter*, 26 June 2015.

[86] Park, '*Crazy Rich Asians* Presents a Whole New Wave of Stereotypes'.

as a man entering into this space directly contrasts with Liane Moriarty's description of herself as 'frustrated by the women's fiction label', seeing it as exclusionary rather than exclusive, and is likewise juxtaposed with the reception of *Big Little Lies* as 'more than' chick lit, discussed later in this Element.[87] *Crazy Rich Asians* has also been categorised as 'wealth porn' or 'lifestyle porn' (a category also used to describe *Big Little Lies*), but Ding coins a new category for *Crazy Rich Asians*: Asian pride porn.

> 'Asian pride porn narratives, such as the *Crazy* series, strategically deploy neoliberal multiculturalist rhetorics, characterized by the conflation of financial success with racial equality, to reimagine diasporic Asian cultural citizenship and romanticize the process of diaspora through global capitalism. The Asian diasporics in Kwan's novels are ideal consumers, whose cosmopolitan status is maintained through the consumption of European, and occasionally American, luxury goods.'[88]

## NW

Our second case study, *NW*, is the fourth novel by award-winning contemporary English novelist Zadie Smith. It was published in 2012 in the UK by Hamish Hamilton (an imprint of Penguin Random House), and in the USA and Australia by Penguin Books. The novel explores the lives of four main characters – Leah, Natalie, Felix, and Nathan – living in the 'NW' postcode area of North West London, each grappling with personal and professional dilemmas that intersect with their class and ethnic backgrounds. *NW* deals with themes of multiculturalism, social class and professional mobility, place, identity, and authenticity. Smith captures the complex and turbulent social, cultural, and political environment in a pre-Brexit Britain.

Smith is from Willesden, a working-class neighbourhood in North West London, has a mixed-heritage background (her father is English

---

[87] C. Tominey, 'Stop Calling Books "Chick Lit", Says *Big Little Lies* Author', *The Telegraph*, 19 October 2018.

[88] Ding, '"Asian Pride Porn"', p. 69.

and her mother is Jamaican), and studied English literature at King's College, Cambridge. Self-representation and themes of class, ethnicity/race, authenticity, and subjecthood have been central to Zadie Smith's writing: these themes are also directly reflected and explored in *NW*. In particular, Smith's 'mixed' heritage – and her straddling of class boundaries – has informed her books and the family sagas she tends to write. Smith has written about how, for her, voice, place, and personal experience are complexly interrelated; in describing her college experiences – moving between Cambridge and Willesden, for example – she explains how 'at home, during the holidays, I spoke with my old voice, and in the old voice seemed to feel and speak things that I couldn't express in college, and vice versa'.[89] We see this type of code-switching in *NW* in how Keisha/Natalie struggles with her different identities; each one is a labour, and she uses the drag metaphor to examine which of her personas is the most authentic:

> 'Daughter drag. Sister drag. Mother drag. Wife drag. Court drag. Rich drag. Poor drag. British drag. Jamaican drag. Each required a different wardrobe. But when considering these various attitudes she struggled to think what would be the most authentic, or perhaps the least inauthentic.'[90]

Smith was catapulted into the literary spotlight at twenty-four, in 2000, when she published her (multi-award-winning) first novel, *White Teeth*. At the time *The Guardian* described her as, 'young, black, British – and the first publishing sensation of the millennium'.[91] In fact, many media descriptions of Smith centre around her age, ethnicity, and appearance: from 'Her beauty, brains, and mixed ethnic background made her a poster girl for Cool Britannia'[92] to the more offensive 'the George Eliot of multiculturalism',

---

[89] Smith, *Ethno-symbolism and Nationalism*, p. 133.

[90] Z. Smith, *NW* (Penguin Press, 2012), p. 333.

[91] S. Merritt, 'She's Young, Black, British – and the First Publishing Sensation of the Millennium', *The Guardian*, 16 January 2000.

[92] B. Kachka, 'Hello, Gorgeous: *On Beauty* by Zadie Smith', *New York Magazine*, 1 September 2005.

'the Lauryn Hill of London Literature', and literature's 'great black hope'.[93] Although Smith has rejected ideas of herself as a spokesperson for multiculturalism,[94] she has influenced a new generation of British authors of colour, as we can see from the quotes cited in what follows.[95] Smith is seen not only as an author but as the 'embodiment of cultural authority and celebrity'.[96]

> 'She's one of the few writers who has been able to write about the London I grew up in, complex, multicultural London, lived-in London; not tourist London, Richard Curtis London where brown or black people barely exist, but my London.'[97]

> 'Zadie's brilliance lies somewhat in the fact that she is so good, one of the most homogenous, male-dominated and white-washed industries in the country has had no choice but to acknowledge her splendour. Here, our most celebrated writers – the ones whose work we annotate and deconstruct at school, the ones whose stories are considered worth the risky business of a print to silver screen transition, the ones whose names are stacked in the various "important people" lists – don't usually look like Zadie Smith. They don't write about the Britain I know, they certainly didn't go to state school and they're rarely women of colour. And yet, with a seat at their very same table, is Zadie, who does and did and is. And that can be a very powerful thing for a young female writer of colour to internalise, even subconsciously.'[98]

---

[93]  A. Edemariam, 'Profile: Zadie Smith', *The Guardian*, 3 September 2005.

[94]  K. Shaw, '"A Passport to Cross the Room": Cosmopolitan Empathy and Transnational Engagement in Zadie Smith's *NW* (2012)', *C21 Literature: Journal of 21st-Century Writings* 5, no. 1 (2017): 1–23.

[95]  M. Bausells, 'In Praise of Zadie Smith's London', *Lit Hub*, 14 December 2016.

[96]  Procter and Benwell, *Reading across Worlds*, p. 151.

[97]  Nikesh Shukla, author and editor of *The Good Immigrant*, quoted in Bausells, 'In Praise of Zadie Smith's London'.

[98]  Yomi Adegoke, writer and co-author of *Slay in Your Lane: The Black Girl Bible*, quoted in Bausells, 'In Praise of Zadie Smith's London'.

> 'It was as though someone had held up a mirror that normal-
> ised my reflection, where once I saw it as ugly and erroneous,
> but now it was beautiful. And it came from a writer so
> accessible, whose world was not too far from my own. I felt
> that perhaps one day I too could do the same.'[99]

As with Smith's other novels, *NW* was published to critical acclaim and was a bestseller in the UK and internationally.[100] *NW* follows the lives of four different characters living in London. The title, *NW*, is the start of the postcode for North West London, where the novel is set. In fact, much of the novel zigzags between the impoverished Willesden, Kilburn (where Smith is from) and the more affluent Queen's Park (where Smith currently lives). This area is known for its multicultural community, which is reflected in the polyphonic nature of the book and ethnic/racial diversity of the main characters. McLeod argues that London 'occupies a particularly significant place in the evolution of postcolonial and oppositional thought and action, and has long been an important site of creativity and conflict for those from countries with history of colonialism'.[101] The experiences of the characters in *NW* are rooted in the city's imperial past and show how communities are constructed there. This type of multicultural community, common in many parts of London, is not without its tensions, as noted in the text when Pauline (Leah's mother) 'looks pointedly towards their old estate, full of people from the colonies and the Russiany lot'.[102]

As noted earlier, London, as with many of Smith's other novels, plays an important role in *NW*. However, in an interview for *The Bookseller*, Smith declared that she is finished writing about the city, despite being one of its

---

[99] J. J. Bola, poet and author of the novel *No Place to Call Home*, quoted in Bausells, 'In Praise of Zadie Smith's London'.

[100] The Penguin UK cover, with its iconic red, white, and blue diamonds, boasts that it is a 'Sunday Times top ten bestseller', while the Penguin US edition, with stark black and red text on a white background, describes it as a 'New York Times bestseller'.

[101] J. McLeod, *Postcolonial London: Rewriting the Metropolis* (Routledge, 2004), p. 6.

[102] Smith, *NW*, p. 77.

better-known chroniclers.[103] Migration and settlement have redefined British national identity and challenged how London, with by far the largest migrant population in the UK, is constituted. Smith has described London as 'a state of mind', and she is one of a group of contemporary authors whose work reflects the changing nature of London and the UK.[104] She dissects London over a period that saw it turn from a prosperous, multi-cultural city to one influenced by a culture of fear after the 7/7 terrorist attack. The 2008–9 financial crisis highlighted the class divide and inequalities in the UK, and research has shown how disparities in income have increased since then.[105] The intersections of ethnicity and class, and the social inequality those identities bring, were never made more evident in recent years than they were by the fire at Grenfell Tower in 2017.[106] David Marcus contends that *NW* is 'a fiction of austerity' – a work of literature that responds (consciously or unconsciously) to the global financial crisis – and is aesthetically different from Smith's previous work, delving deeper into inequality, social class, and identity.[107]

## Big Little Lies

Our third case study title is *Big Little Lies*. Published in 2014 by Pan Macmillan Australia and in the USA and UK by Penguin Random House, it is the sixth novel by Sydney-based author Liane Moriarty. Following the international success of her fifth book, *The Husband's Secret*, in 2013, the highly anticipated *Big Little Lies* was the first Australian title to debut at number one on the *New York Times* bestseller list. It has also subsequently been adapted as an HBO series starring Nicole Kidman, Reese Witherspoon,

[103] A. O'Keeffe, 'Zadie Smith: "I Wanted to Express How It Is to Be in the World As a Black Woman"', *The Bookseller*, 8 November 2016.

[104] S. Hughes, 'Zadie Smith: The Smart and Spiky Recorder of a London State of Mind', *The Observer*, 6 November 2016.

[105] R. Partington, 'How Unequal Is Britain and Are the Poor Getting Poorer?' *The Guardian*, 5 September 2018.

[106] A. Gentleman, 'Grenfell Tower MP Highlights Huge Social Divisions in London', *The Guardian*, 13 November 2017.

[107] D. Marcus, 'Post-hysterics: Zadie Smith and the Fiction of Austerity', *Dissent*, 60, no. 2 (2013): 67–73 (p. 67).

and Shailene Woodley. The book tells the story of three women – Jane, Madeline, and Celeste – all mothers to children attending kindergarten at Pirriwee Public School in Sydney's affluent and mostly mono-ethnic Northern Beaches.[108]

By contrast with *NW* and *Crazy Rich Asians*, its main characters predominantly straddle the middle and upper classes, with the exception of single working mother Jane, who has recently moved to Pirriwee. The book's descriptions of nationality and ethnicity are limited to peripheral working-class characters: the 'young married Korean couple'[109] who clean Celeste's house and the 'French nanny' who works for one of the schoolyard parents. There's also a euphemistic racialisation of the barista, Tom, as non-white: 'His skin during the autumn was the colour of a weak latte. During the summer it was the colour of a hot chocolate.'[110]

Snobbishness about wealth and ethnicity pervade the book. For example, when Jane replaces a lost class toy, one of the mothers reflects: 'That cheap synthetic toy she replaced it with smelled just terrible. Made in China. The hippo's face wasn't even friendly.'[111] Despite this, characters in the book consider the area diverse in terms of wealth and occupation:

> We've got a lot of tradies in Pirriwee. Like my Stu. Salt of the earth. Or salt of the sea, because they all surf of course. Most of the tradies grew up here and never left. Then you've got your alternative types. Your dippy hippies. And in the last ten years or so, all these wealthy execs and banker wankers have moved in and built massive McMansions up on the cliffs. But! There's only one primary school for all our kids! So at school events you've got a plumber, a banker and a crystal healer standing around trying to make conversation. It's hilarious.[112]

---

[108] Australian Bureau of Statistics, 'Sydney – Northern Beaches. General Community Profile', 2016 Census of Population and Housing, 2017.
[109] L. Moriarty, *Big Little Lies* (Penguin, 2014), p. 169.
[110] Moriarty, *Big Little Lies*, p. 229. [111] Moriarty, *Big Little Lies*, p. 150.
[112] Moriarty, *Big Little Lies*, p. 168.

In stark contrast to representations of, for example, Smith's multicultural London, Samantha, one of the schoolyard mothers in *Big Little Lies*, sees diversity in a combination of self-starting, independent tradespeople, white-collar workers, and people with the privilege to choose 'alternative life-styles'. A few pages later, the very wealthy Celeste describes the families in the area as occupying 'different levels of comfortable'.[113] Crucially, both descriptions portray an area that is overwhelmingly affluent.

The book explores themes of abuse, trauma, assault, and violence, hand in hand with those of women's friendship, family, and community, and it was critically acclaimed for its balancing of 'serious' themes with a 'chick lit' style.[114] In an all-encompassing feature about Liane Moriarty for the *Sydney Morning Herald*'s 'Good Weekend' liftout, Amanda Hooton introduces Moriarty as 'the most successful author you've never heard of that this country has ever seen'.[115] Hooton, based on an interview with Moriarty, explores how she has been pigeonholed as an author of chick lit, suggesting this is the cause of her lack of critical attention despite a large readership. Like the American reviewers of *Big Little Lies*, Hooton homes in on Moriarty's balance between the serious and the insubstantial, describing the book as 'commercial fiction ... But it contains surprisingly dark elements – damage, death, viciousness – that are deeply unsettling amid the Tupperware parties and banana muffin baking'.[116]

Thematically, the TV series mirrors the book, and key plot points relating to abuse, domestic violence, and the central murder remain the same; the setting, however, is drastically changed to coastal Monterey, California. The specificity of the original setting clearly does not figure as a key part of the book's international critical reception. The *New York Times* critic Janet Maslin describes it as 'set on a scenic peninsula outside Sydney, Australia, near one of the world's most beautiful beaches (perhaps Bondi)',

---

[113] Moriarty, *Big Little Lies*, p. 171.

[114] J. Maslin, 'How Was School? Deadly', *New York Times*, 24 July 2014;
L. Greenblatt,'*Big Little Lies*', *Entertainment Weekly*, 7 August 2014.

[115] A. Hooton, 'How Sydney Author Liane Moriarty Sold Six Million Books and Inspired an HBO Series', *Sydney Morning Herald*, 15 July 2016.

[116] Hooton, 'How Sydney Author Liane Moriarty Sold Six Million Books'.

a bizarre suggestion for any readers familiar with Sydney.[117] By contrast, Ella Donald's review for *The Guardian*, which was prompted by the release of the adaptation, describes the book as 'indebted to its specific location' with *Big Little Lies* 'lauded for being uncomfortably recognisable . . . full of knowing humour about the first year of school in a Sydney beach suburb'.[118] Australia does not have a central position in the international book market like the USA and UK do, despite being a large anglophone nation; Driscoll and Rehberg Sedo found that 'bestsellers' national origins are usually disregarded by media and reader reviews', noting that 'nationality is all but "washed out" of the print media reception of transnational bestsellers'.[119] This is also consistent with observations that Australian readers demonstrate less interest or attachment to an Australian setting in a popular fiction text than they do in a literary fiction text.[120] We likewise found that this seems to be the case with reviews of *Big Little Lies*, particularly because the Australian books that achieve international bestseller status are those whose settings are either international or generic enough to be familiar to audiences in the UK or USA.[121] We see this phenomenon with the adaptation of Moriarty's work.

## *Distribution*

Sales figures are notoriously slippery, particularly with the rise of digital sales, but they provide a starting point for comparing the distribution of each of our case study titles. Overall, the USA book market in 2017 reported

---

[117] Maslin, 'How Was School? Deadly'.

[118] E. Donald, 'Has the Satire and Humour of *Big Little Lies* Been Lost in Translation?' *The Guardian*, 22 March 2017.

[119] Driscoll and Rehberg Sedo, 'The Transnational Reception of Bestselling Books', p. 252.

[120] P. Buckridge, 'Readers and Reading', in *Paper Empires: A History of the Book in Australia, 1946–2005*, edited by C. Munro and R. Sheahan-Bright, pp. 344–81 (University of Queensland Press, 2006), p. 354.

[121] C. Parnell and B. Driscoll, 'Institutions, Platforms and the Production of Debut Success in Contemporary Book Culture', *Media International Australia* 187, no. 1 (2023): 123–38; Driscoll and Rehberg Sedo, 'The Transnational Reception of Bestselling Books'.

approximately 687,200,000 units sold, making it around 3.5 times the size of the UK market, at 190,600,000 units, and slightly less than 12.5 times the size of the Australian market, at 55,500,000 units.[122] Patterns of whole-of-life unit sales (all of which were accessed on 4 October 2018, but for commercial reasons, not all of which can be published here) for *Big Little Lies* and *Crazy Rich Asians* to a certain extent reflect the sizes of the three markets. Unit sales of each in the UK were proportionally small in relation to market size, with 206,771 copies of *Big Little Lies* and only 23,533 copies of *Crazy Rich Asians* sold. The USA dominates in sales. Even considering the proportional 3.5 times in sales for the US compared to the UK given the ratio in market size *Big Little Lies* unit sales were nearly an additional 2 times larger, with *Crazy Rich Asians* sales even more disproportionally large – more than 5 times larger. Unit sales of *Crazy Rich Asians* in Australia directly reflected its market size comparison with the US, while sales of *Big Little Lies* were proportionally high, at just under a third of USA unit sales. Sales for *NW*, by contrast, were strongly configured by nation, with UK unit sales, at 146,702, nearly 1.8 times those in the US and more than 16 times those in Australia. The sales figures for each title, in each of our three key markets, are, in other words, large but varied. Each is considered a bestseller, but the numbers behind the bestseller status are affected by the country of origin and the attachment of each to literary and popular modes.[123]

## *Goodreads Demographics*

To what extent do these sales convert into online conversations? The amount of attention each text has received on Goodreads, seen in the total number of ratings and reviews given to each title, is collated in Table 1. The number of ratings and reviews is broadly in proportion to these texts' sales figures.

[122] These were the figures NPD BookScan/Nielsen BookScan reported in these three territories: see J. Milliot, 'Print Sales Up Again in 2017', *Publishers Weekly*, 5 January 2018; A. Flood, '"Leading the Entertainment Pack": UK Print Book Sales Rise Again', *The Guardian*, 4 January 2019; Books+Publishing, 'The Market Down Under', *Books+Publishing*, 2 October 2018.

[123] M. Pouly, 'Playing Both Sides of the Field: The Anatomy of a "Quality" Bestseller', *Poetics* 59 (2016): 20–34.

Table 1 Popularity on Goodreads

|  | *Crazy Rich Asians* | *NW* | *Big Little Lies* |
|---|---|---|---|
| Number of Goodreads ratings | 214,204 | 28,787 | 571,343 |
| Number of Goodreads reviews | 21,695 | 3,173 | 39,136 |

According to a 2015 study, the average star rating given to books on Goodreads is 3.88.[124] *Crazy Rich Asians'* overall star rating of 3.83 comes close to matching this; *Big Little Lies* is above average at 4.25, with *NW* significantly below average, with an average star rating of 3.44.

Goodreads reviews and reviewers' data enabled us to explore the book cultures that have grown around these three texts. We collected the publicly viewable 5-star, 4-star, 3-star, 2-star, and 1-star reviews shown by default by Goodreads for each text, giving us balanced corpora of close to 1,500 reviews for each text. Where reviewers made their demographic information – location, age, and gender – publicly accessible, we collected this too, giving us an overall picture of the demographic breakdown of the major online reception of each text. As noted earlier (in Chapter 2), we have endeavoured to follow the evolving best-practice guidelines at all times in collecting these data; all demographic data are aggregated and only top-level, publicly viewable data were accessed.

Table 2 shows the level of reporting of demographic information between Goodreads reviewers. Reviewers of each book are more likely to report nationality than any other demographic data, then age, and least likely to report gender. Reviewers of *NW* are the most exceptional: they are the most likely to report nationality and by far the least likely to report

---

[124] S. Dimitrov, F. Zamal, A. Piper, and D. Ruths, 'Goodreads versus Amazon: The Effect of Decoupling Book Reviewing and Book Selling,' *Proceedings of the International AAAI Conference on Web and Social Media* 9, no. 1 (2015): 602–5.

Table 2 Reporting of Demographic Information on Goodreads

|  | *Crazy Rich Asians* | *NW* | *Big Little Lies* |
|---|---|---|---|
| Gender | 9.76% | 2.94% | 7.79% |
| Age | 30.01% | 25.23% | 30.43% |
| Nationality | 63.50% | 72.16% | 66.93% |

Table 3 Reported Gender of Reviewers on Goodreads

|  | *Crazy Rich Asians* | *NW* | *Big Little Lies* |
|---|---|---|---|
| Woman | 9.29% | 2.00% | 7.07% |
| Men | 0.47% | 0.93% | 0.71% |

gender identity, which – as we will see shortly – is consistent with the framing and themes of many of the reviews themselves.

Gender identity on Goodreads overall is heavily skewed towards women, with approximately three-quarters of all members with gender recorded identifying as women.[125] Apart from each being skewed towards women reviewers, none of the texts are typical in this regard, as can be seen in Table 3. At one end of the scale, reviewers of *Crazy Rich Asians* are nearly twenty times as likely to identify as women as they are as men, and reviewers of *Big Little Lies* are nearly ten times as likely; at the other end, the small number of *NW* reviewers who report their gender identity are approximately one-third men and two-thirds women: this is less of a gender divide than the population of Goodreads overall. Existing research into Goodreads demographics has found 'that there is little difference between male and female users in patterns of behaviour, except for females registering more books and rating them less positively'. While this may be the case for the population overall, we hypothesise that the

[125] M. Thelwall and K. Kousha, 'Goodreads: A Social Network Site for Book Readers', *Journal of the Association for Information Science and Technology* 68, no. 4 (April 2017): 972–83.

Table 4 Reported Age of Reviewers on Goodreads

|  | *Crazy Rich Asians* | *NW* | *Big Little Lies* |
|---|---|---|---|
| 18–25 | 7.55% | 3.20% | 5.21% |
| 26–35 | 13.24% | 9.15% | 12.43% |
| 36–45 | 6.08% | 5.94% | 6.36% |
| 46–55 | 1.80% | 3.20% | 2.93% |
| 56–65 | 1.00% | 2.00% | 2.00% |
| 66–75 | 0.20% | 1.47% | 1.07% |
| 76+ | 0.13% | 0.27% | 0.43% |

substantial proportional differences between reviewers' reported genders for these titles are likely to be closely linked to the titles' audience demographics outside of Goodreads, which in turn is configured by titles' perceived genre and associated marketing, and key features of the titles including character and author demographics.

Reviewer age for all three titles (Table 4) peaks in the relatively young twenty-six to thirty-five age bracket. This peak is least marked for reviewers of *NW*, who are more likely to be slightly older than those for *Big Little Lies* and *Crazy Rich Asians*.

The final demographic information we interrogate is reviewer nationality. Table 5 shows the percentage of reviewers who report as coming from the USA, the UK, Canada, or Australia for the three titles (these being the largest readerships explicitly identified in the data sets). Notably, while *NW* sold far more copies (in absolute as well as proportional terms) in the UK, like *Crazy Rich Asians* and *Big Little Lies*, its Goodreads reviewership is substantially a North American one. *Crazy Rich Asians*, despite selling nearly twice as many copies in Australia as in the United Kingdom, receives similar amounts of Goodreads attention from Australian and British reviewers.

It is possible that this is based on the sampling technique that we have of necessity used – that of accessing the reviews and reviewers that Goodreads makes available. Goodreads' default view is based on an

Table 5 Reported Location of Reviewers on Goodreads: Major Anglophone
Markets

|  | *Crazy Rich Asians* | *NW* | *Big Little Lies* |
|---|---|---|---|
| USA | 38.90% | 40.32% | 36.57% |
| United Kingdom | 2.41% | 12.75% | 3.86% |
| Canada | 5.82% | 3.74% | 5.57% |
| Australia | 1.94% | 2.67% | 4.00% |

unknown, 'black box' algorithm, but seems to consistently show a mixture
of reviews that have been well 'liked', reviews by known authors, and
some recent reviews; in other words, it seems to rely at least in part on
mechanisms that privilege reviewers with high levels of existing social and
cultural capital within the site. Goodreads caters to an international
audience but with a strong USA inflection: 220 million of its 435 million
monthly page views are from the USA.[126] Particularly given Goodreads'
commercial relationship to the USA book industry superpower Amazon,
it is possible that its algorithmic features overemphasise North American
users even when not representative. There is no way to examine this
algorithm and its inner workings without Amazon's permission, an unli-
kely possibility given how closely Amazon guards its data from others –
industry professionals and academics alike. In order to be transparent
about the power of algorithms in shaping reader experience and reviews, it
is worth acknowledging this very real possibility. Despite this, looking in
depth at the 'long tail' of other represented nationalities emphasises the
diversity of Goodreads' national make-up. Table 6 shows the ten countries most commonly reported among our reviewers following the four
major anglophone countries in Table 5; after the additional ten nations
listed in Table 6, another eighty-one nationalities appear in the data set.
This particular snapshot chart also demonstrates *Crazy Rich Asians*'
unsurprisingly higher number of Singaporean, Indonesian, Filipino, and
Indian reviewers.

[126] Goodreads, 'Book Discovery Information Kit.'

Table 6 Reported Location of Reviewers on Goodreads: Other Markets

|  | *Crazy Rich Asians* | *NW* | *Big Little Lies* |
|---|---|---|---|
| Indonesia | 1.47% | 0.13% | 0.79% |
| Netherlands | 0.33% | 1.13% | 0.71% |
| India | 0.80% | 0.60% | 0.64% |
| Spain | 0.27% | 0.93% | 0.79% |
| Singapore | 1.54% | 0.27% | 0.14% |
| Philippines | 1.54% | 0.07% | 0.07% |
| New Zealand | 0.40% | 0.67% | 0.57% |
| Brazil | 0.47% | 0.27% | 0.79% |
| France | 0.60% | 0.47% | 0.36% |
| Ireland | 0.27% | 0.47% | 0.57% |
| Italy | 0.33% | 0.60% | 0.36% |

## Identity in Online Discussion

The quantitative and demographics-based approaches we have just discussed answer some of our questions: how have these bestselling books travelled, and with what kinds of internationalised communities of discourse do they resonate? They demonstrate the importance of data-rich research for mapping broader trends in the movement of different types of books across national boundaries and into international commercially and socially inflected literary spaces. In doing so, they also raise questions, in particular: what of the specific book cultures each title has generated? We explore this using summative content analysis of the text of the Goodreads reviews. We generated lists of frequent terms using the program NVivo, explored these terms in context within the corpus, and also used this process to identify specific reviews for further close reading. Excerpted quotes from some of these reviews included in the analysis have been selected as particularly illustrative of important patterns, and while we critically engage with these perspectives, we have also aimed to give sufficient quotations to accurately convey readers' own thoughts. In doing so, we reiterate and take seriously the principle, discussed earlier in this Element, that 'readers' own statements about their reading are worth paying attention to', and invite our own readers to take their time with the thoughts of the readers of our three case study novels.[127]

Our analysis of the Goodreads reviews for *NW*, *Crazy Rich Asians*, and *Big Little Lies* is grouped around four main themes that emerged from our content analysis: representation and misrepresentation, genre and gender identity, author–reader relationships, and adaptation and format.

## Representation and Misrepresentation

Race or ethnicity, class, and gender feature prominently as themes in our three case study texts, and the representation (or misrepresentation) of certain groups, particularly marginalised communities, comes through in the reviews of the novels. Readers see themselves in the books and also understand different points of view. In reviews of *NW*, the words 'class' and 'race' or 'ethnicity' are often paired, with readers acknowledging the intersectional identities of the characters ('You could read some third-rate theorising about the intersectionality of race, gender and class. Or you could read this book, and actually learn something' and 'Zadie Smith has written a dark, entertaining meditation on race, class and society in the modern melting pot'). Two reviewers – both white men – very explicitly disclose their ethnicities in order to preface their comments (one positive, one negative). The positive reviewer highlights that the book gave him, as a white man, a better understanding into a different world. The negative reviewer uses his ethnicity to position his dislike/lack of understanding of the book. This reviewer mentions accessibility – that is, he was unable to understand some of the nuances of the book, which focuses on migrant communities in London. Another reviewer took umbrage at reading perspectives different from their own, particularly those that look at the harsher realities of life in London:

> The author depicts life in Kilburn North London (NW) in an
> incredibly depressing way. I actually found it quite distasteful
> and some of the story line (not that there is much of one)

[127] Driscoll and Rehberg Sedo, 'Faraway, So Close', p. 248.

> completely unnecessary. I could be very naive and not open
> to understanding different perspectives but this is not the
> reason I read books. I think the author is still riding on the
> back of her unusual name and *White Teeth*'s success.

There are racist undertones in this review, in particular the suggestion that she is exploiting both her heritage (signified by the 'unusual name') and the success of her first novel, the acclaimed and multi-award-winning *White Teeth*. (It is worth noting that *NW* is Smith's fourth book; two award-winning books were published between *White Teeth* and *NW*.) On the other hand, one reviewer praised Smith for helping them confront their own biases, even if it was uncomfortable for them. 'Smith's work challenged me both technically and emotively and forced me to confront my personality and biases as a reader – I am immensely grateful to her for that.' Another noted that sharing a similar background to the characters in the book helped with their understanding. 'I think if you come from a certain background, as a city dweller, you'll empathise with the characters.' Those who connected to the characters (an important driver in literary fiction) – one reviewer said, 'characters are wonderfully flawed and interesting' – showed an understanding of the multicultural nature of London: 'I feel like I can see [NW London] through the eyes of her characters; she captures the cadence and speech-patterns of a broad swathe of London's immigrant denizens, irish, caribbean, caribbean-italian, algerian, maybe-indian, russian, tempered by the toughness of the council estates, smoothed out by education and desire, full of slang and peculiarities.'

Representation is a double-edged sword in the reviews of *Crazy Rich Asians*. On the one hand, some readers are happy about 'Asia', 'Asian' people, and 'Asian fiction' being represented, even, at times, in spite of not liking the book. However, there are also concerns about misrepresentations and stereotyping. The fact that Kwan is an 'Own Voices' author – he was born in Singapore, moved to the USA as a child, and is/was part of the Singaporean wealthy elite – is picked up by some reviewers both in a positive and negative way.[128]

---

[128] 'Own Voices', a term coined by Corinne Duyvis, is when an author shares a marginalised identity or identities with the protagonist in their book/s. The

In a few instances, Kwan is compared to Amy Tan and her famous, canonical Asian American title *The Joy Luck Club*: 'This book reminds me of Amy Tan's *Joy Luck Club* only updated with a whole lot of family drama and a splash of Asian humour.'

The book is set in Singapore and is largely about Singaporean culture, although other Asian cultures are represented in the book, and not always in the most positive way. For example, one reviewer complained, 'I'm Malaysian and even I couldn't get used to the slang . . . Totally fine with foreigners who read the book and give them a slight taste of Singapore culture. But what I'm not fine with is butchering my ethnic language – Malay.' It is easy, perhaps, to conflate representation of Singaporean culture and identity with broader East and Southeast Asian representation (especially since the title is *Crazy Rich Asians*). Readers' ethnicities were more closely linked to those within the book. For example, readers explicitly identified as Asian American, Chinese, Singaporean, Taiwanese, and Malaysian. Only one reviewer explicitly identified as white in the content of the review. For one Singaporean reviewer, despite not giving the book high praise on its writing, plot, and character merits, the reviewer felt a need to recommend the book solely based on the fact that it represents Singapore when so few other books do ('However, being a Singaporean, I feel as though I should actively promote this for the amount of Asian representation and how it revolves around my country'). In other words, the book's existence as a title depicting Singaporean identity is a significant factor for this reader, even before the manner of representation of specific characters and cultures in the content of the book is considered.

People from Taiwan and Mainland China, and Chinese Americans are all described in a derogatory way by the characters in the text, as noted by many reviewers, particularly those who share characters' ethnic

argument is that 'Own Voice' authors write from their lived experiences and from insider perspectives, which reinforces the authenticity of their writing. However, the term has been problematised since it was co-opted by corporate publishers and used as a marketing tool. The term has also been used to police the identities of authors.

backgrounds. For example, one Taiwanese American reviewer expressed their annoyance at gendered stereotypes in *Crazy Rich Asians*: 'As a Taiwanese American I had to bristle pretty much any time Taiwanese women were mentioned as being the gold-digger types.' This type of identity disclosure, where readers include their ethnicity in the reviews, could be more common for *NW* and *Crazy Rich Asians* because they are books by and about Black people and people of colour. There is a dearth of books about socially marginalized groups, particularly by 'Own Voice' authors, so readers/reviewers (who share those marginalisations) may be more likely to self-identify publicly when they see themselves reflected in the books. White readers and reviewers might not disclose such information because literature typically features white characters and thus their identities are (and have been) often reflected on the page.[129] Even when the information about characters and authors is not readily disclosed, the default is for readers to assume whiteness; by extension, readers who don't disclose and discuss their ethnicity in the reviews may also be assuming whiteness.

Discussion of representation and misrepresentation is not as significant in reviews of *Big Little Lies*, likely because the characters are relatively homogenous: predominantly middle- to upper-class, women, white, and living in Sydney. Interestingly, however, in the adaptation of the book into an HBO series (discussed later in this Element), a casting choice was made that increased the racial diversity of the cast; central character Bonnie Carlson is played by Zoë Kravitz. She is the sole Black actress, indeed the only person of colour, in the TV series, but Goodreads reviewers did not comment on this.

## Genre and Gender Identity

While all three books are fictional, contemporary, family-centred novels, Goodreads reviews illustrate the contrasting ways that readers see *NW* as 'literary fiction', whereas *Crazy Rich Asians* and *Big Little Lies* are perceived as more gendered and middlebrow, usually described as 'women's fiction' or 'chick lit', and *Crazy Rich Asians* is additionally considered 'romance'. While reviewers of *NW* do not tend to classify the book using the term

[129] Ramdarshan Bold, *Inclusive Young Adult Fiction*.

'literary fiction', readers acknowledge that because Smith has won many prestigious prizes and awards, there is an expectation of social commentary and superior writing style. Many reviewers expressed uncertainty and lack of confidence in their opinions of *NW*, using words such as 'quite' to qualify their remarks – feeling that they *should* understand and enjoy the book because of the author's acclaim. This is aligned with the observation from Procter and Benwell that readers in book groups feel a moral obligation and accountability to other members of their reading groups.[130] For Goodreads reviewers of *NW*, readers communicate a moral obligation to read and understand such an influential and important text, prefacing or apologising when they do not finish the book or understand it 'properly'. Since literary fiction does not follow any genre convention or formula, is not plot driven, and often relies on symbolism, such books, and the experience of reading them, can be more ambiguous for their readers. For example, one reviewer compared it to poetry. 'Reading this book was more like reading a poem, you have to pay attention to what the writer is trying to say, it is somewhat cryptic.' Others explicitly stated how difficult the book was to read and how that impacted their reading experience: 'This book was so hard to follow'; 'That book was exhausting'; 'I found this book unaccessible, and put it down'. Some reviewers acknowledged Smith's talent. 'Yes, you're very clever, Zadie, but books have to be readable.' Going back to the assumed non-conventional nature of literary fiction, which is typically more character driven than plot driven, it was interesting to read this review. 'I love Zadie Smith, and the writing as always started out great, but I just wasn't hooked enough by the plot.'

Based on our data, there is a clear distinction between reading middlebrow or popular fiction and literary fiction (i.e. reading for enjoyment versus reading for a challenge or to learn), particularly when we look at the reviews of *NW*. These often include rereading, persevering, and not quitting in order to fully understand and appreciate the book. For example, one reviewer wrote, 'Not so much a review, as a tip: Once you've read the book, go back and read the first two chapters again. They take on a richer meaning once you've been with the characters for a bit. It all ends up feeling quite

[130] Procter and Benwell, *Reading across Worlds*.

circular – in a really interesting way.' Even starting *NW* requires a certain level of confidence for some readers. Driscoll argues that feminisation is one of the characteristics of the literary middlebrow and this certainly is demonstrated in the reviews and categorisations of *Big Little Lies* and *Crazy Rich Asians* on Goodreads.[131] Unlike reviews of *NW*, which avoid classifying the book as literary, a number of reviewers explicitly describe *Crazy Rich Asians* as 'chick lit', 'romance', and 'rom-com'. The top categorisations for *NW* – apart from 'to-read' and 'currently reading', both of which are similar to *Big Little Lies* and *Crazy Rich Asians* – are the more generic 'fiction', 'contemporary', and 'novels.' In fact, there are many different, sometimes derogatory, value judgements of *Crazy Rich Asians*, which put the book in a particular category of (mostly lowbrow) entertainment. These include comparisons to TV series like *Gossip Girl* and *Sex and the City*. Likewise, *Big Little Lies* is regularly described as 'quaint', 'fluff', 'silly', and 'dribble'. One reviewer expressed their disappointment in a gendered review. 'I was disappointed by this frothy and superficial story about a group of gossipy moms.' Other gendered terms used often in the reviews include: 'mama drama' (frequently compared to *Desperate Housewives*), 'women's lit', and 'angsty suburban drama'.

Indeed, reader expectations based on the genre of *Big Little Lies* come through in many readers' assertion that it is explicitly *not* 'chick lit' or is somehow different or better, distancing themselves from the categorisation. One reviewer, who makes clear that they are not a 'chick lit' reader, mentioned the serious themes in the book that distinguish it from other books of the same genre:

> It's an unabashed beach read that handles serious subject matter fairly for 430 pages. I'm not the beach-read type but don't like to discount a book when I have fair warning that I'm not the intended audience, the amount of pink on the cover was enough of a clue, to say nothing of the pithy jacket copy and provocative titles of Moriarty's bibliography. Having

[131] B. Driscoll, *The New Literary Middlebrow: Tastemakers and Reading in the Twenty-First Century* (Springer, 2014).

slogged through sensationalistic paperbacks on plenty of sandy shores, I was pleased to find that this longwinded not-mystery-genre-mystery was the very rare, socially-conscious variety of fluff.

Domestic abuse is a central theme in *Big Little Lies*, and many reviewers express surprise about the seriousness of this theme in a 'chick lit' novel. The term 'trigger warning' preambles several reviews to let review readers know that uncomfortable themes (primarily domestic abuse) are perhaps unexpectedly present.

This 'chick lit' categorisation is a barrier to overcome for some readers, such as a reader who did not expect to like the story because for 'some unknown reason I was sure that Liane Moriarity is a chick-lit writer'. Some reviewers embraced the categorisation, calling it a 'guilty pleasure' ('Liane Moriarty is my guilty pleasure. Her books and writing style are not substantial, but her characters are colourful and intriguing and you want to know more about them the more you read. She is *Cosmopolitan* in book form'), while one man wore the chick lit badge proudly:

> I'll do my best to churn out a review here but my eyes are still a bit bleary from devouring the end of this one. Oddly enough, this is a book that my wife is so surprised I liked. She loved it, and a lot to do with that is that she is a junior kindergarten teacher and she certainly related to just about everything in this. Well, she forgets that a lot to do with me enjoying a book is terrific character development and engaging story. And really, how can anyone resist a story about the cliques and infighting among the parents of kindergarteners? I'm pretty sure I enjoyed it more than she did. I'm sure I was raving about it to her much more often than she was to me. Wow, does Liane Moriarty have it. She's very widely read by women of course, since her main characters are women, but you fellas out there take heed: this is solid storytelling in a domestic setting and anyone sloughing this off as chick lit can do so at your own peril. No wonder

Stephen King is a fan. Both *The Husband's Secret* and *Big Little Lies* could have easily come from his word processor, simply for the skilled characterization and ability to hook the reader into a story. Both of these have mysteries at their core, and the fun of them is waiting for the slow reveals and watching the characters cope with them. Discovering this lady has been the highlight of my reading so far this year. Absolutely outstanding. And hell, if this means I'm a chick-litre [sic] then so be it, I'm all in with Moriarty.

Just as genres involve a set of expectations between the reader and author, the reading experience is also shaped by different expectations for particular authors. While Smith and *NW* received some criticisms that the book and Smith's writing diverged from the more upbeat *White Teeth*, Moriarty's work is criticised as repetitive: 'This book is just about the same as all of Liane Moriarty's book. Set in Australia, About mums with problems . . . It is the third that my book club has read and I am done reading this author. I need something new and not just the same story again.'

We can see the constructions of genre play out here: there are expectations on Smith to create similar work to *White Teeth*, despite literary fiction not following any particular norms. Moriarty, who does follow some conventions in her work, which has been called everything from 'chick lit' to 'domestic noir', is expected to change her 'domestic' focused and place-based narratives.

Similarly, there is an overarching sense that *Crazy Rich Asians* is throwaway fiction that does not need to be reread. This is counter to reviews of *NW*, where rereading is common practice to fully understand the book. Many reviewers find *Crazy Rich Asians* funny and entertaining; we found that this was the antithesis of responses to *NW*, where reviewers find the book to be 'hard' (the sixtieth most frequent word in the *NW* reviews). Genre expectations are communicated by some of the comments about how expectations for a 'chick lit' novel were met, exceeded, or challenged. As we have already noted, wealth is an important theme and plot point in *Crazy Rich Asians*, and reviews link the book to traditional British culture such as Jane Austen novels and the *Downton Abbey* television series, which portray archetypal and well-known models of family drama, family values, traditions, class, wealth, and snobbery. These comparisons were common in a number of published newspaper reviews of the book (including in venues like the *Washington Post* and *Guardian*), and this recirculates in the Goodreads reviews, with twenty-four reviewers in our data set explicitly comparing the novel to Austen's work, and six comparisons to *Downton Abbey*. This offers an example of how attachment to a more established elite cultural product is used as a touchstone to position and qualify the book in both mainstream and social media discussion.

## Author–Reader Relationship

Perceptions of the relationship between author and reader differ among the three titles. Readers of *NW* acknowledge the high symbolic and cultural capital (although not put in those terms) of Zadie Smith, and the prestige and critical acclaim associated with her work. Reviewers mentioned the various accolades Smith has won over the years, including the Women's Prize for Fiction, being a *Sunday Times* bestseller, being shortlisted for the Booker, and the Orange Prize. This perceived prestige was met in different ways. For example, one reviewer felt intimidated: '*NW* has been sitting on my bookshelf, intimidating me, for a couple years.' Another review acknowledged the accolades in their polite but negative review: 'this is a very well-respected book that I never quite warmed to'. Reviewers who call *NW* a 'book' rather than a 'novel' are more likely to be negative about the readability and difficulty of the writing or themes, suggesting a different type of readership. However, even in these negative reviews, when reviewers criticise the 'book', they are hesitant to criticise Smith herself. Many reviewers read *NW* because of Zadie Smith's authorial brand, voice, prestige, and overall symbolic capital but do not always enjoy the themes covered (as noted in the latter quote just cited). Readers have a certain expectation about Smith's books, as we can see from this review: 'For some reason I wanted to like this book. Its awards and write ups were quite favourable and the subject matter appealed to me. However, in the end, I was disappointed.'

Overall, many reviewers took responsibility for their lack of understanding rather than placing the onus on Smith:

> 'Sadly, not as good as what I was led to believe by her popularity and the critics. It might mean that I lack some understanding of the culture, never having lived in or visited NW London.'

> 'I really struggled with this book. On one hand I know that Zadie Smith is much smarter than I'll ever be. But this writing all went over my head. I appreciate that she was trying to do something here. She was writing a new kind of novel. Round, dynamic, complex characters. A story of place. Something that speaks to humanity. But I just couldn't get it.'

Many reviewers mention Smith's award-winning debut novel *White Teeth* as a comparison to *NW*, often painting *NW* in a more negative light (especially in contrast to the more humourous or lighter nature of *White Teeth* and its optimistic view of multiculturalism). However, these reviewers also failed to acknowledge how much more fraught racial tensions in the UK have become since 2000, so it is inevitable that Smith's work would pick up on and reflect these growing tensions.

When reviewers of *Crazy Rich Asians* discuss the author, they are generally very positive, particularly with regard to his authenticity and detail. There is less of an established relationship, unlike with Zadie Smith and her previous work, since this was Kwan's debut novel. The fact that Kwan is an Own Voices author – from Singapore and from a wealthy background – helps to elevate his perceived authenticity in the eyes of readers. The representation of East and Southeast Asians and Asian Americans is not only rare but also different to many other portrayals in popular media, and this frequently inflects readers' experiences of the book. One reviewer enthused about such representation. 'It was also really fun to see into the lives of wealthy Asians as their wealth is always under-represented compared to white billionaires.' Even if the review was not so positive, there is still recognition of the book being more representative, as one reviewer states, 'Honestly this was pretty appalling pulp fiction except at least it wasn't about white people.' As noted previously, reading representative literature can result in reviewers divulging their ethnicity or nationality. One reviewer reveals, 'I am Singaporean, so getting to witness a story based in my country is so exciting. So proud and thankful for Kevin Kwan for writing this bad boy.' However, there are still concerns about stereotypes, as one reviewer stresses. 'I'm glad that this book is bringing more attention to the Asian community – though I hope people don't generalise too much about crazy rich Asians!'

Liane Moriarty, much like Zadie Smith, was often known by readers because they had been exposed to her previous works. However, readers display less loyalty and reverence towards Moriarty as an author than towards Zadie Smith. Some readers enjoyed Moriarty's previous works, which prompted them to read *Big Little Lies*, while others read *Big Little Lies* despite not loving some of Moriarty's other works (particularly *The Husband's Secret*). However, many readers who reviewed *Big Little Lies* negatively express disappointment as a result of enjoying her previous works. *Big Little Lies*, along with Moriarty's previous books, is a popular choice for book clubs, frequently appearing on recommended book club lists on Goodreads. *Big Little Lies* was a book club choice for several of the reviewers – for example, one reviewer wrote, 'I read this only because it was my book club's pick for the month, I would not have read it voluntarily otherwise.' This type of peer-to-peer recommendation is a different pattern of recommendation and taste-making to a book like *NW*. While literary prizes and recommendations by cultural elites confer symbolic value on a book such as *NW*, book clubs and their choices are firmly grounded in middlebrow reading practices.[132]

In their own analysis of Goodreads reviews, Driscoll and Rehberg Sedo note the importance of the review space to the author–reader relationship:

> [T]he Goodreads review is another space where readers negotiate their sense of proximity to authors. Reviews can invoke intimacy by mentioning the author, a process that some media theorists would see as para-sociality or, in Rojek's (2016) term, presumed intimacy, since there is no physical relationship between the author and reader. But when viewed from the standpoint of readers, a review that mentions an author forms a connection, a link in a network.

[132] Driscoll, *The New Literary Middlebrow*.

> The review is of an authored book, not just a book; the
> author is part of an intimate reading experience. A little
> more than 20% (20.1%) of the reviews explicitly mention the
> author, either by name or indirectly.[133]

The author is indeed a part of the intimate reading experience for reviewers
of *NW*, *Crazy Rich Asians*, and *Big Little Lies* on Goodreads, where loyalty
to the author is intertwined with the author's identities (nation, race,
gender), prestige, and the perceived authenticity of these identities in
interaction with the text.

## Adaptation and Format

The last current of discussion in the reviews of these three books relates to
adaptation or format, particularly audiobook and film or TV adaptations. In
the publishing industries more generally, audiobooks have seen tremendous
growth in the past ten years. While point-of-sale data is generally not
collected for audio titles through traditional routes, estimates and survey-
based studies point to revenue growth in 2021 in the USA of 25 per cent and
in the UK of 13 per cent.[134] Reviewers' discussion of adaptation and format,
whether audio, televisual, or filmic, relates very closely to their perceptions
of place and identity.

---

[133] Driscoll and Rehberg Sedo, 'Faraway, So Close', p. 255 citing C. Rojek,
*Presumed Intimacy: Parasocial Interaction in Media, Society and Celebrity Culture*
(Polity, 2016).

[134] For further discussion of recent growth in the audiobook market, see
T. Osborne, 'Audiobooks on the Rise As More Australians Plug into Stories on
Smartphones', *ABC*, 3 July 2017; P. Anderson, 'Audio Publishers Association
Reports a 22.7-Percent Jump in 2017 Revenue', *Publishing Perspectives*,
20 June 2018; 'Audio "Booming" with 13% Growth Last Year', *The Bookseller*,
11 March 2019; M. Weber, 'On Audiobooks and Literature in the Post-digital
Age', *Overland*, 3 October 2019; M. Weber, '"Reading" the Public Domain:
Narrating and Listening to Librivox Audiobooks', *Book History* 24, no. 1 (2021):
209–43; and M. Weber, R. Giblin, Y. Ding, and F. Petitjean-Hèche, 'Exploring
the Circulation of Digital Audiobooks: Australian Library Lending 2006–2017',
*Information Research* 26, no. 2 (2021).

The audiobook gave particular national and regional grounding to the reading experience for many reviewers, and audiobook mentions were overwhelmingly positive. One reviewer of *NW* highlights how the different regional accents – and class distinctions – are particularly prevalent in the audio versions. 'The narrators are outstanding, nailing all of the different accents and cadences of working class and immigrant Brit speech.' Language, race, and class come to the surface with reviews of the audiobook as an immersive and authentic experience: 'listening to an audiobook with narrators who effortlessly switch dialects helps' and it was 'a delight to hear this story read by two English people who can render Smith's writing in dialect and vernacular into the voices that she is imitating'. Similarly, reviewers of *Crazy Rich Asians* also appreciate the accents in the audiobook adaptation. One reviewer explains that they 'listened to the audiobook for this one and Lynn Chen does a fantastic job of not only imitating at least [a] dozen accents (ranging from British to Malaysian) but making it easy to discern between the crazy amount of characters by her voice alone. Someone get the woman a Tony or an Oscar or something'.

Although all three books have been adapted into either film or TV series, discussion of film and TV adaptation was most prominent in reviews of *Crazy Rich Asians*, followed by discussion of the HBO series of *Big Little Lies* (with only four of the reviews for *NW* mentioning its BBC adaptation). For *Crazy Rich Asians*, for example, 'movie' is the fourteenth most frequently used word in the review corpus overall. Some readers heard about the film first and read the book as a result. Many preferred the film to the book, or if they did not enjoy the book still wanted to see the film. However, not all reviewers were positive, particularly when it came to representation: 'I just wish the first Asian American Hollywood film in twenty-five years would be closer to its predecessor, *The Joy Luck Club*, than to this trainwreck source material.'

*Crazy Rich Asian*s is visually rich and highly descriptive: it is, in other words, already cinematic in the way it is constructed. It is also highly place-based. Singapore is an important part of the plot but less of a 'character' than London is in *NW* (it is the twentieth most frequently used word in *Crazy Rich Asians*' reviews, while London was the eleventh most frequently used word in *NW*'s reviews). Readers unfamiliar with the country added comments about how much they learned about Singapore, and those who had visited appreciated reading about aspects of the country that they recognised: 'One reason that I enjoyed this book was because this is a world that I have no knowledge of.' Many reviewers expressed that *Crazy Rich Asians* gave them the opportunity to travel vicariously to Singapore and other places. This is categorically not present in the reviews of *NW*, which is mostly set in a working-class area – not one usually featured in travel guides about London and its attractions.

Much like *Crazy Rich Asians*, the adaptation of *Big Little Lies*, this time into an HBO TV series, features in the reviews. Some reviewers found the book after watching the HBO series, while others read the book first. Readers unsurprisingly discuss the differences between the two, often indicating that they enjoyed the book more than the series: 'I am watching the series now, I have already some troubles with the casting and so far the book is better.' The well-known actresses Reese Witherspoon and Nicole Kidman are frequently mentioned, with certain readers prompted to watch the HBO series primarily on the prestige and love of these actresses. As we noted before, the HBO series eliminates the Australian setting, lifting the story and putting it in Monterey, California. In fact, some reviewers, influenced by the adaptation, describe the book itself as set in California: 'Well-paced murder mystery which takes place in a small, wealthy California beach town'. It is unclear, in such reviews, whether the reviewer is writing about the book or the series. Such reviewers might not have read the book at all, but wanted to be seen as a reader on Goodreads and therefore published a review based on the TV series. Another possibility is that in the multimodal, cross-media consumption of the twenty-first-century reader, a reviewer may have both read the book and watched the series but mixed up some of the particulars and differences between the representations in the review. Given the prevalence of cross-media consumption and discovery, the storyworlds are not as distinct as one might think.[135]

The many mentions of these various adaptations (audiobook, film, and television series) of the novels support what Procter and Benwell found in their

---

[135] R. Noorda and K. Berens, 'Immersive Media & Books: Consumer Behavior and Experience with Multiple Media Forms', *PDX Scholar*, 2021.

transnational book group research: 'Our book groups regularly draw analogies with film and television series, and use electronic media to animate and extend their conversations from the printed page. New technologies might be said to augment rather than erode reading cultures in this context.'[136] We argue that new technologies and other media (film, TV, audiobooks) do more than only *augment* reading culture; they can even become *interchangeable* with reading culture, such that reviewers of the book on Goodreads cannot distinguish the film or series from the book. Goodreads discussions about and reception of *Crazy Rich Asians*, *Big Little Lies*, and *NW*, in relation to TV, film, and audio adaptations, illustrate the interconnected nature of media forms and consumption.

[136] Procter and Benwell, *Reading across Worlds*, p. 58.

## 4 Conclusion

What is the relationship between books and nations during the contemporary shifts towards international business models, social and cultural interactions, and growing conservative nationalism? And how can we best explore this relationship?

In this Element, we have examined the international reception of three novels of family-centred fiction by three very different authors writing across genres. Our examination is rooted in our argument that reading in the twenty-first century is triply situated: within the self, within the nation, and within the online environment. There were many ways in which the reading experience of these three texts was situated: online within Goodreads, within each author's own national context and identity, and in a large and interconnected media ecosystem that encompasses print, digital, and audiobooks, in addition to film, television, and social platforms.

Key to our investigation in this Element is identity: what conceptions of identity are being (and not being) articulated in relation to the reception of books and to what extent does this interact with, overlap, or exceed concepts of nation? Gender identity, race/ethnicity, and nationality resurfaced frequently in readers' discussions of the texts and their reactions to and relationships with the setting, characters, and authors. Additionally, while all of the Goodreads reviewers had read these texts in some capacity, they varied in their identity as 'readers'; some perceived and portrayed themselves as 'serious' readers, while others (sometimes apologetically) identified themselves as leisurely, non-professional readers.

While all of these identities present varying levels of complexity for each individual, national identity is one of the most complicated. These readers still carry identities related to nation, but often individuals identify with more than one nation. Diaspora and increased mobility have not done away with national identity; rather, the number of national identities to which an individual may connect with and identify has increased. Place matters in reader reception. And yet, in considering the role of place, we must not ignore online spaces as 'places': places of connection, places of building and sharing various readerly identities, and places that – like any physical place – are mediated.

The centre–periphery binary does not map so easily when nation, genre, and race are layered on to the space of online book culture. Each of the three titles, for example, sold proportionally best in their home market; despite Australia being a 'peripheral' market, *Big Little Lies* sold the largest number of units proportional to the national book market. Thus sales are strongly configured by nation, most prominently for *NW*, where sales in the UK far surpassed those in the USA and Australia. The national identity of Goodreads reviewers for particular titles does not proportionally match sales, however. Despite prominent sales in the UK for *NW*, North America was the location of the largest proportion of *NW* reviewers on Goodreads, for example.

Readers use national, racial, and gender identity to frame their reviews and position themselves in the conversation; this seems to be truer for literary fiction and novels with strong national, racial, and gender themes (like *NW*). Just as it has become important for 'Own [Voice] Authors' writers to identify themselves as such to readers, readers also identify themselves as 'Own Readers' to each other in the reviews.

Our data also reveal the fluid nature of cross-media consumption habits. Format and adaptation do not only augment reading culture and the reading experience; they at times are interchangeable to readers in their reviews.

There is a need for more investigations of reading that are situated in multiple ways. While this Element has examined three anglophone case studies of texts from the US, the UK, and Australia, this research is part of a larger project to examine place and national identity in relation to book reception throughout the anglophone publishing world. The next stages for this project include broadening its locational scope to move outside the US, the UK, and Australia; broadening its textual scope to include more closely comparative case studies; and broadening its methodological scope in order to decouple its exploration of book cultures from specific texts entirely.

In summary, we find that national identity and readers' expression of it are connected to other aspects of their identities. These various facets of identity inform and shape the reading experience. But the expression of these identities is complex and unequal, sometimes requiring readers to perform certain identities and obscure others, national identity among them. Because the online environment is international but individual, readers still bring their own national identities and contexts; flagging, concealing, or negotiating of national identity may be required in online reading communities. We see how some readers reveal their own national identities to other readers to validate their perspectives on the text (Own Readers), while others conceal this information in their reviews of the books. The sociopolitical environment, national identity of the author, and themes of the book all factor into a reader's decision to reveal or conceal national identity in reviews. The relationship between place, identity, and textual culture simultaneously persists and is problematised in the twenty-first century, and this Element sets the terms of a broader, ongoing conversation about how this will continue to play out.

# Bibliography

Abad-Santos, Alexander. 'Why Asians Love *Crazy Rich Asians*'. *The Atlantic*, 4 September 2013. https://bit.ly/48RaBDS.

Ackland, Robert. *Web Social Science: Concepts, Data and Tools for Social Scientists in the Digital Age*. Sage, 2013.

Ahmad, Piotr. 'Digital Nationalism As an Emergent Subfield of Nationalism Studies: The State of the Field and Key Issues'. *National Identities* 24(4): 307–17.

Allington, Daniel. '"Power to the Reader" or "Degradation of Literary Taste"? Professional Critics and Amazon Customers As Reviewers of *The Inheritance of Loss*'. *Language and Literature* 25, no. 3 (1 August 2016): 254–78. https://doi.org/10.1177/0963947016652789.

Anderson, Benedict. *Imagined Communities: Reflections on the Origin and Spread of Nationalism*. Verso, 1983.

Anderson, Porter. 'Audio Publishers Association Reports a 22.7-Percent Jump in 2017 Revenue'. *Publishing Perspectives*, 20 June 2018. https://bit.ly/3vnZHaV.

The Association of Internet Researchers (AOIR). 'Internet Research: Ethical Guidelines 3.0', 6 October 2019. https://aoir.org/reports/ethics3.pdf.

Australian Bureau of Statistics. 'Sydney – Northern Beaches: General Community Profile'. 2016 Census of Population and Housing, 2017. www.abs.gov.au/census/find-census-data/community-profiles/2016/122.

Bartlett, Lesley, and Frances Vavrus. *Rethinking Case Study Research: A Comparative Approach*. Taylor & Francis, 2016.

Bausells, Marta. 'In Praise of Zadie Smith's London'. *Lit Hub*, 14 December 2016. https://lithub.com/in-praise-of-zadie-smiths-london.

Berry, Chris, So-yŏng Kim, and Lynn Spigel. *Electronic Elsewheres: Media, Technology, and the Experience of Social Space*. University of Minnesota Press, 2010.

Billig, Michael. *Banal Nationalism*. Sage, 1995.

Books+Publishing. 'The Market Down Under'. *Books+Publishing*, 2 October 2018. https://bit.ly/49VQoy1.

The Association of Internet Researchers (AOIR). 'Internet Research: Ethical Guidelines 3.0', 6 October 2019. https://aoir.org/reports/ethics3.pdf.

The Bookseller. 'Audio "Booming" with 13% Growth Last Year.' *The Bookseller*, 11 March 2019. https://bit.ly/4chzSdc.

Brouillette, Sarah. *Postcolonial Writers in the Global Literary Marketplace*. Palgrave Macmillan, 2007.

Buckridge, Patrick. 'Readers and Reading'. In *Paper Empires: A History of the Book in Australia 1956–2005*, edited by Craig Munro and Robyn Sheahan-Bright, pp. 344–81. University of Queensland Press, 2006.

Carter, David. 'After Postcolonialism'. *Meanjin* 66, no. 2 (2007): 114–19. https://bit.ly/3IF7wvT.

Casanova, Pascale. *The World Republic of Letters*. Harvard University Press, 2004.

de Certeau, Michel. 'Reading As Poaching'. In *The Practice of Everyday Life*, translated by Stephen Rendall, pp. 165–76. University of California Press, 1984.

Cheney-Lippold, John. 'A New Algorithmic Identity: Soft Biopolitics and the Modulation of Control'. *Theory, Culture & Society* 28, no. 6 (2011): 164–81.

Chiu, Allyson. 'Is *Crazy Rich Asians* Historic? "That's Just Way Too Much Pressure," Says Kevin Kwan, Who Wrote the Book'. *Washington Post*, 13 August 2018. https://wapo.st/3PnZ5sW.

Cramer, Florian. 'What Is "Post-Digital"?' In *Postdigital Aesthetics: Art, Computation and Design*, edited by David M. Berry and Michael Dieter, pp. 12–26. Palgrave Macmillan, 2015. https://doi.org/10.1057/978113 7437204_2.

Deahl, Rachel, and Jim Milliot. 'Amazon Buys Goodreads'. *Publishers Weekly*, 28 March 2013. https://bit.ly/3PlFKZ2.

Dimitrov, Stefan, Faiyaz Zamal, Andrew Piper, and Derek Ruths 'Goodreads versus Amazon: The Effect of Decoupling Book Reviewing and Book Selling'. *Proceedings of the International AAAI Conference on Web and Social Media* 9, no. 1 (2015): 602–5. https://doi.org/10.1609/icwsm.v9i1.14662.

Ding, Yuan. '"Asian Pride Porn": Neoliberal Multiculturalism and the Narrative of Asian Racial Uplift in Kevin Kwan's *Crazy Rich Asians* Trilogy'. *MELUS* 45, no. 3 (2020): 65–82.

Dixon, Robert. 'Australian Literature: International Contexts'. *Southerly* 67, no. 1/2 (2007): 15–27.

Donald, Ella. 'Has the Satire and Humour of *Big Little Lies* Been Lost in Translation?' *The Guardian*, 22 March 2017. https://bit.ly/3vcecPc.

Driscoll, Beth. *The New Literary Middlebrow: Tastemakers and Reading in the Twenty-First Century*. Springer, 2014.

Driscoll, Beth, and DeNel Rehberg Sedo. 'Faraway, So Close: Seeing the Intimacy in Goodreads Reviews'. *Qualitative Inquiry* 25, no. 3 (1 March 2019): 248–59. https://doi.org/10.1177/1077800418801375.

Driscoll, Beth, and DeNel Rehberg Sedo. 'The Transnational Reception of Bestselling Books between Canada and Australia'. *Global Media and Communication* 16, no. 2 (2020a): 243–58.

Driscoll and C. Squires, *The Frankfurt Book Fair and Bestseller Business.*, Cambridge University Press; 2020, p. 6.

Edemariam, Aida. 'Profile: Zadie Smith'. *The Guardian*, 3 September 2005. www.theguardian.com/books/2005/sep/03/fiction.zadiesmith.

Eisenstein, Elizabeth L. *The Printing Press As an Agent of Change, Volume 1*. Cambridge University Press, 1980.

Ellis-Pedersen, Hannah, and Lily Kou. 'Where Are All the Brown People? Crazy Rich Asians Draws Tepid Response in Singapore'. *The Guardian*, 21 August 2018. https://bit.ly/3ICOUN0.

Finn, Ed. 'Revenge of the Nerd: Junot Díaz and the Networks of American Literary Imagination'. *Digital Humanities Quarterly* 7, no. 1 (1 July 2013). www.digitalhumanities.org/dhq/vol/7/1/000148/000148.html.

Fish, Stanley. *Is There a Text in This Class? The Authority of Interpretive Communities*. Harvard University Press, 1980.

Fishkin, Shelley Fisher. 'Crossroads of Cultures: The Transnational Turn in American Studies. Presidential Address to the American Studies Association, 12 November 2004'. *American Quarterly* 57, no. 1 (2005): 17–57. https://doi.org/10.1353/aq.2005.0004.

Flood, Alison. '"Leading the Entertainment Pack": UK Print Book Sales Rise Again'. *The Guardian*, 4 January 2019. https://bit.ly/43lGVh5.

Fraser, Robert, and Mary Hammond. *Books without Borders, Volume 1: The Cross-National Dimension in Print Culture*. Palgrave Macmillan, 2008. https://bit.ly/43mVSzC.

Fuller, Danielle. 'The Multimodal Reader: Or, How My Obsession with NRK's Skam Made Me Think Again about Readers, Reading and Digital Media'. *Participations: Journal of Audience and Reception Studies* 16, no. 1 (2019): 496–509.

Fuller, Danielle, and DeNel Rehberg Sedo. *Reading beyond the Book: The Social Practices of Contemporary Literary Culture*. Routledge, 2013.

Genette, Gerard. *Paratexts: Thresholds of Interpretation*. Cambridge University Press, 1997.

Gentleman, Amelia. 'Grenfell Tower MP Highlights Huge Social Divisions in London'. *The Guardian*, 13 November 2017. https://bit.ly/3TnehY6.

Goodreads. 'Book Discovery Information Kit'. n.d. www.goodreads.com/advertisers.

Greenblatt, Leah. 'Big Little Lies'. *Entertainment Weekly*, 7 August 2014. https://ew.com/article/2014/08/07/big-little-lies.

Griswold, Wendy. *Regionalism and the Reading Class*. University of Chicago Press, 2008. http://ebookcentral.proquest.com/lib/anu/detail .action?docID=408434.

Gruzd, Anatoliy, and DeNel Rehberg Sedo. '#1b1 t: Investigating Reading Practices at the Turn of the Twenty-First Century'. *Mémoires Du Livre* 3, no. 2 (8 June 2012). https://doi.org/10.7202/1009347ar.

Hall, Geoff. 'Texts, Readers – and Real Readers'. *Language and Literature* 18, no. 3 (2009): 331–7.

Henningsgaard, Per. 'Ebooks, Book History, and Markers of Place'. *Logos* 30, no. 1 (6 June 2019): 31–44. https://doi.org/10.1163/18784712-03001005.

Henningsgaard, Per. 'The Editing and Publishing of Tim Winton in the United States'. In *Tim Winton: Critical Essays*, edited by Lyn McCredden and Nathanael O'Reilly, pp. 122–60. UWA Publishing, 2014.

Henningsgaard, Per. 'Emerging from the Rubble of Postcolonial Studies: Book History and Australian Literary Studies'. *Ilha Do Desterro* 69, no. 2 (2016): 117–26. https://doi.org/10.5007/2175-8026.2016v69n2p117.

Hookway, Nicholas. '"Entering the Blogosphere": Some Strategies for Using Blogs in Social Research'. *Qualitative Research* 8, no. 1 (2008):91–113. https://doi.org/10.1177/1468794107085298.

Hooton, Amanda. 'How Sydney Author Liane Moriarty Sold Six Million Books and Inspired an HBO Series'. *Sydney Morning Herald*, 15 July 2016. https://rb.gy/mbi09d.

Hughes, Sarah. 'Zadie Smith: The Smart and Spiky Recorder of a London State of Mind'. *The Observer*, 6 November 2016. https://rb.gy/va6sl8.

Jacklin, Michael. 'The Transnational Turn in Australian Literary Studies'. *Journal of the Association for the Study of Australian Literature*. Special Issue: Australian Literature in a Global World (2009): 1–14. https://openjour nals.library.sydney.edu.au/index.php/JASAL/article/view/10040.

Jay, Paul. *Global Matters: The Transnational Turn in Literary Studies*. Cornell University Press, 2011.

Kachka, Boris. 'Hello, Gorgeous: *On Beauty* by Zadie Smith'. *New York Magazine*, 1 September 2005. http://nymag.com/guides/fallpreview/2005/books/12856.

Kwan, Kevin. *Crazy Rich Asians*. Anchor, 2013.

Langer, Roy, and Suzanne C. Beckman. 'Sensitive Research Topics: Netnography Revisited'. *Qualitative Market Research* 8, no. 2 (2005): 189–203.

Li, Xiufang, and Juan Feng. 'Security and Digital Nationalism: Speaking the Brand of Australia on Social Media'. Media International Australia (2022): 1329878X221139581.

Marcus, David. 'Post-hysterics: Zadie Smith and the Fiction of Austerity'. *Dissent* 60, no. 2 (1 March 2013): 67–73. https://doi.org/10.1353/dss.2013.0035.

Maslin, Janet. 'How Was School? Deadly'. *New York Times*, 24 July 2014. https://rb.gy/11w8ln.

McLeod, John. *Postcolonial London: Rewriting the Metropolis*. Routledge, 2004.

McMullen, Jeff. 'Indigenous Australia Is the True Foundation of Our Multicultural Society'. *The Guardian*, 6 August 2015. https://rb.gy/03z6k2.

Merritt, Stephanie. 'She's Young, Black, British – and the First Publishing Sensation of the Millennium'. *The Guardian*, 16 January 2000. www.theguardian.com/books/2000/jan/16/fiction.zadiesmith.

Miall, David S. 'Empirical Approaches to Studying Literary Readers: The State of the Discipline'. *Book History* 9 (2006): 291–311. www.jstor.org/stable/30227393.

Mihelj, Sabina, and César Jiménez-Martínez, 'Digital Nationalism: Understanding the Role of Digital Media in the Rise of "New" Nationalism'. *Nations and Nationalism* 27, no. 2 (2021): 331–46.

Milliot, Jim. 'Print Sales Up Again in 2017'. *Publishers Weekly*, 5 January 2018. https://rb.gy/76uam0.

Moriarty, Liane. *Big Little Lies*. Penguin, 2014.

Murray, Simone. 'Secret Agents: Algorithmic Culture, Goodreads and Datafication of the Contemporary Book World'. *European Journal of Cultural Studies* 24, no. 4 (2021): 970–89.

Noorda, Rachel. 'From *Waverley* to *Outlander*: Reinforcing Scottish Diasporic Identity through Book Consumption'. *National Identities* 20, no. 4 (2018): 361–77.

Noorda, Rachel, and Kathi Inman Berens. 'Immersive Media & Books: Consumer Behavior and Experience with Multiple Media Forms'. *PDX Scholar* (2021): https://pdxscholar.library.pdx.edu/eng_fac/74.

Noorda, Rachel, and Stevie Marsden. 'Twenty-First Century Book Studies: The State of the Discipline'. *Book History* 22 (2019): 370–97. https://doi.org/doi:10.1353/bh.2019.0013.

O'Keeffe, Alice. 'Zadie Smith: "I Wanted to Express How It Is to Be in the World As a Black Woman."' *The Bookseller*, 8 November 2016. https://shorturl.at/rBOQ4.

Osborne, Tegan. 'Audiobooks on the Rise As More Australians Plug into Stories on Smartphones'. *ABC*, 3 July 2017. https://shorturl.at/crvL2.

Park, Patricia. '*Crazy Rich Asians* Presents a Whole New Wave of Stereotypes.' *The Guardian*, 3 September 2013. https://shorturl.at/glwyB.

Parnell, Claire, and Beth Driscoll. 'Institutions, Platforms and the Production of Debut Success in Contemporary Book Culture'. *Media International Australia* 187, no. 1 (2023): 123–38.

Partington, Richard. 'How Unequal Is Britain and Are the Poor Getting Poorer?' *The Guardian*, 5 September 2018. https://shorturl.at/rwI29.

Pickford, Susan. 'The Booker Prize and the Prix Goncourt: A Case Study of Award-Winning Novels in Translation'. *Book History* 14 (2011): 221–40. www.jstor.org/stable/41306537.

Pink, Sarah, and Kerstin Leder Mackley. 'Saturated and Situated: Expanding the Meaning of Media in the Routines of Everyday Life'. *Media, Culture & Society* 35, no. 6 (1 September 2013): 677–91. https://doi.org/10.1177/0163443713491298.

Ponzanesi, Sandra. *The Postcolonial Cultural Industry: Icons, Markets, Mythologies*. Palgrave Macmillan UK, 2014. https://doi.org/10.1057/9781137272591.

Pouly, Marie-Pierre. 'Playing Both Sides of the Field: The Anatomy of a "Quality" Bestseller'. *Poetics* 59 (2016): 20–34.

Procter, James, and Bethan Benwell. *Reading across Worlds: Transnational Book Groups and the Reception of Difference*. Palgrave Macmillan, 2014.

Ramdarshan Bold, Melanie. *Inclusive Young Adult Fiction: Authors of Colour in the United Kingdom*. Palgrave Pivot, 2019. https://doi.org/10.1007/978-3-030-10522-8.

Rehberg Sedo, DeNel. 'Readers in Reading Groups: An Online Survey of Face-to-Face and Virtual Book Clubs'. *Convergence* 9, no. 1 (2003): 66–90.

Rehberg Sedo, DeNel. 'Richard & Judy's Book Club and "Canada Reads": Readers, Books and Cultural Programming in a Digital Era'. *Information, Community and Society* 11, no. 2 (2008): 188–206.

Rodger, Nicola. 'From Bookshelf Porn and Shelfies to #bookfacefriday: How Readers Use Pinterest to Promote Their Bookishness'. *Participations: Journal of Audience and Reception Studies* 16, no. 1 (2019): 473–94.

Rojek, Chris. *Presumed Intimacy: Parasocial Interaction in Media, Society and Celebrity Culture*. Polity, 2016.

Rosenblatt, Louise M. 'The Literary Transaction: Evocation and Response'. *Theory into Practice* 21, no. 4 (1982): 268–77. www.jstor.org/stable/1476352.

Sapiro, Gisèle. 'How Do Literary Works Cross Borders (Or Not)? A Sociological Approach to World Literature'. *Journal of World Literature* 1, no. 1 (2016): 81–96.

Scanlon, Christopher. 'Bogans and Hipsters: We're Talking the Living Language of Class'. *The Conversation*, 24 February 2014. https://short url.at/klnG8.

Shaw, Kristian. '"A Passport to Cross the Room": Cosmopolitan Empathy and Transnational Engagement in Zadie Smith's *NW (2012)*'. *C21 Literature: Journal of 21st-Century Writings* 5, no. 1 (2017): 1–23.

Smith, Anthony D. *Ethno-Symbolism and Nationalism: A Cultural Approach*. Routledge, 2009.

Smith, H. Jeff, Tamara Dinev, and Heng Xu. 'Information Privacy Research: An Interdisciplinary Review'. *MIS Quarterly* 35, no. 4 (2011): 989–1016. https://doi.org/10.2307/41409970.

Smith, Zadie. *Changing My Mind: Occasional Essays*. Penguin Press, 2009. http://archive.org/details/goldenhillsofwes00paxs.

Smith, Zadie. *NW*. Penguin Press, 2012.

Steiner, Ann. 'Private Criticism in the Public Space: Personal Writing on Literature in Readers' Reviews on Amazon'. *Participations: Journal of Audience and Reception Studies* 52, no. 2 (2008). www.participations.org/Volume%205/Issue%202/5_02_steiner.htm.

Stratoudaki, Hara. 'Greek National Identity on Twitter: Re-negotiating Markers and Boundaries'. *National Identities* 24, no. 4 (2022): 319–35.

Sugiura, Lisa, Rosemary Wiles, and Catherine Pope. 'Ethical Challenges in Online Research: Public/Private Perceptions'. *Research Ethics* 13, no. 3–4 (2017): 184–99. https://doi.org/10.1177/1747016116650720.

Sun, Rebecca. '*Crazy Rich Asians* Author Kevin Kwan: "Why Does Hollywood Think We'd Want to See This Movie with White People?"' *The Hollywood Reporter*, 26 June 2015. https://tinyurl.com/354e39ad.

Thelwall, Mike, and Kayvan Kousha. 'Goodreads: A Social Network Site for Book Readers'. *Journal of the Association for Information Science and Technology* 68, no. 4 (April 2017): 972–83. https://doi.org/10.1002/asi.23733.

Tominey, Camilla. 'Stop Calling Books "Chick Lit", Says *Big Little Lies* Author'. *The Telegraph*, 19 October 2018. https://tinyurl.com/3neftkbz.

Tynan, Caroline. 'Nationalism in the Age of Social Media'. *Temple Libraries' Scholars Studio* (2017).

Weber, Millicent. *Literary Festivals and Contemporary Book Culture*. Palgrave Macmillan, 2018.

Weber, Millicent. 'On Audiobooks and Literature in the Post-Digital Age'. *Overland*, 3 October 2019. https://overland.org.au/2019/10/on-audiobooks-and-literature-in-the-post-digital-age.

Weber, Millicent. '"Reading" the Public Domain: Narrating and Listening to Librivox Audiobooks'. *Book History* 24, no. 1 (2021): 209–43.

Weber, Millicent, Rebecca Giblin, Yanfang Ding, and François Petitjean-Hèche. 'Exploring the Circulation of Digital Audiobooks: Australian Library Lending 2006–2017'. *Information Research* 26, no. 2 (2021). http://informationr.net/ir/26-2/paper899.html.

Whitlock, Gillian, and Roger Osborne. '*Benang*: A Worldly Book'. *Journal of the Association for the Study of Australian Literature* 13, no. 3 (2013): 1–15. https://search-proquest-com.virtual.anu.edu.au/docview/1537584145/fulltextPDF/B5B9E34C9552453CPQ/1?accountid=8330.

Wiles, Rosemary. *What Are Qualitative Research Ethics?* Bloomsbury Academic, 2013.

Wilkins, Kim, Beth Driscoll, and Lisa Fletcher. *Genre Worlds: Popular Fiction and 21st-Century Book Culture*. University of Massachusetts Press, 2022.

Willis, Ika. *Reception*. Routledge, 2017.

Yin, Robert K. *Case Study Research: Design and Methods*. Sage, 2009.

**Cambridge Elements** $\equiv$

# Publishing and Book Culture

SERIES EDITOR
## Samantha Rayner
*University College London*

Samantha Rayner is Professor of Publishing and Book Cultures at UCL. She is also Director of UCL's Centre for Publishing, co-Director of the Bloomsbury CHAPTER (Communication History, Authorship, Publishing, Textual Editing and Reading) and co-Chair of the Bookselling Research Network.

ASSOCIATE EDITOR
## Leah Tether
*University of Bristol*

Leah Tether is Professor of Medieval Literature and Publishing at the University of Bristol. With an academic background in medieval French and English literature and a professional background in trade publishing, Leah has combined her expertise and developed an international research profile in book and publishing history from manuscript to digital.

## About the Series

This series aims to fill the demand for easily accessible, quality texts available for teaching and research in the diverse and dynamic fields of Publishing and Book Culture. Rigorously researched and peer-reviewed Elements will be published under themes, or 'Gatherings'. These Elements should be the first check point for researchers or students working on that area of publishing and book trade history and practice: we hope that, situated so logically at Cambridge University Press, where academic publishing in the UK began, it will develop to create an unrivalled space where these histories and practices can be investigated and preserved.

**Cambridge Elements** ≡

# Publishing and Book Culture

BESTSELLERS

## Gathering Editor: Beth Driscoll

Beth Driscoll is Associate Professor in Publishing and Communications at the University of Melbourne. She is the author of *The New Literary Middlebrow* (Palgrave Macmillan, 2014), and her research interests include contemporary reading and publishing, genre fiction and post-digital literary culture.

## Gathering Editor: Lisa Fletcher

Lisa Fletcher is Professor of English at the University of Tasmania. Her books include *Historical Romance Fiction: Heterosexuality and Performativity* (Ashgate, 2008) and *Popular Fiction and Spatiality: Reading Genre Settings* (Palgrave Macmillan, 2016).

## Gathering Editor: Kim Wilkins

Kim Wilkins is Professor of Writing and Deputy Associate Dean (Research) at the University of Queensland. She is also the author of more than thirty popular fiction novels.

Printed in the United States
by Baker & Taylor Publisher Services